Experimenting with Everyday Science

Art and Architecture

Experimenting with Everyday Science

Experimenting with Everyday Science

Art and Architecture

Stephen M. Tomecek

CHELSEA HOUSE
PUBLISHERS

An imprint of Infobase Publishing

In memory of Leonardo, Raphael, Michelangelo, and Donatello—four great masters who not only inspired countless artists, but also served as role models for four equally impressive ninja turtles.

Experimenting with Everyday Science: Art and Architecture

Copyright © 2010 by Infobase Publishing

Chelsea House
An imprint of Infobase Publishing
132 West 31st Street
New York NY 10001

Library of Congress Cataloging-in-Publication Data
Tomecek, Steve.
  Art and architecture / by Stephen M. Tomecek.
    p. cm. — (Experimenting with everyday science)
  Includes bibliographical references and index.
  ISBN 978-1-60413-168-0 (hardcover)
 1. Art and science—Juvenile literature. 2. Architecture and science—Juvenile literature. 3. Art—Study and teaching—Activity programs. 4. Architecture—Study and teaching—Activity programs. 5. Materials—Experiments. I. Title. II. Series.
  N72.S3T66 2010
  701'.03—dc22   2009030195

Chelsea House books are available at special discounts when purchased in bulk quantities for businesses, associations, institutions, or sales promotions. Please call our Special Sales Department in New York at (212) 967-8800 or (800) 322-8755.

You can find Chelsea House on the World Wide Web at http://www.chelseahouse.com

Text design by Annie O'Donnell
Cover design by Alicia Post
Composition by Mary Susan Ryan-Flynn
Cover printed by Bang Printing, Brainerd, MN
Book printed and bound by Bang Printing, Brainerd, MN
Date printed: June 2010
Printed in the United States of America

10 9 8 7 6 5 4 3 2 1

This book is printed on acid-free paper.

All links and web addresses were checked and verified to be correct at the time of publication. Because of the dynamic nature of the Web, some addresses and links may have changed since publication and may no longer be valid.

Contents

Introduction

When you hear the word *science*, what's the first thing that comes to mind? If you are like most people, it's probably an image of a laboratory filled with tons of glassware and lots of sophisticated equipment. The person doing the science is almost always wearing a white lab coat and probably is looking rather serious while engaged in some type of experiment. While there are many places where this traditional view of a scientist still holds true, labs aren't the only place where science is at work. Science can also be found at construction sites, on a basketball court, and at a concert by your favorite band. The truth of the matter is that science is happening all around us. It's at work in the kitchen when we cook a meal, and we can even use it when we paint a picture. Architects use science when they design a building, and science also explains why your favorite baseball player can hit a homerun.

In **Experimenting with Everyday Science**, we are going to examine some of the science that we use in our day-to-day lives. Instead of just talking about the science, these books are designed to put the science right in your hands. Each book contains about 25 experiments centering on one specific theme. Most of the materials used in the experiments are things that you can commonly find around your house or school. Once you are finished experimenting, it is our hope that you will have a better understanding of how the world around you works. While reading these books may not make you a world-class athlete or the next top chef, we hope that they inspire you to discover more about the science behind everyday things and encourage you to make the world a better place!

Safety Precautions

REVIEW BEFORE STARTING ANY EXPERIMENT

Each experiment includes special safety precautions that are relevant to that particular project. These do not include all the basic safety precautions that are necessary whenever you are working on a scientific experiment. For this reason, it is necessary that you read and remain mindful of the General Safety Precautions that follow.

Experimental science can be dangerous, and good laboratory procedure always includes carefully following basic safety rules. Things can happen very quickly while you are performing an experiment. Materials can spill, break, or even catch fire. There will be no time after the fact to protect yourself. Always prepare for unexpected dangers by following the basic safety guidelines during the entire experiment, whether or not something seems dangerous to you at a given moment.

We have been quite sparing in prescribing safety precautions for the individual experiments. For one reason, we want you to take very seriously every safety precaution that is printed in this book. If you see it written here, you can be sure that it is here because it is absolutely critical.

Read the safety precautions here and at the beginning of each experiment before performing each activity. It is difficult to remember a long set of general rules. By rereading these general precautions every time you set up an experiment, you will be reminding yourself that lab safety is critically important. In addition, use your good judgment and pay close attention when performing potentially dangerous procedures. Just because the text does not say "be careful with hot liquids" or "don't cut yourself with a knife" does not mean that you can be careless when boiling water or punching holes in plastic bottles. Notes in the text are special precautions to which you must pay special attention.

GENERAL SAFETY PRECAUTIONS

Accidents caused by carelessness, haste, insufficient knowledge, or taking an unnecessary risk can be avoided by practicing safety procedures and being alert while conducting experiments. Be sure to check the individual experiments in this book for additional safety regulations and adult supervision requirements. If you will be working in a lab, do not work alone. When you are working off site, keep in groups with a minimum of three students per group, and follow school rules and state legal requirements for the number of supervisors required. Ask an adult supervisor with basic training in first aid to carry a small first-aid kit. Make sure everyone knows where this person will be during the experiment.

PREPARING

- Clear all surfaces before beginning experiments.
- Read the instructions before you start.
- Know the hazards of the experiments and anticipate dangers.

PROTECTING YOURSELF

- Follow the directions step-by-step.
- Do only one experiment at a time.
- Locate exits, fire blanket and extinguisher, master gas and electricity shut-offs, eyewash, and first-aid kit.
- Make sure there is adequate ventilation.
- Do not horseplay.
- Keep floor and workspace neat, clean, and dry.
- Clean up spills immediately.
- If glassware breaks, do not clean it up; ask for teacher assistance.
- Tie back long hair.
- Never eat, drink, or smoke in the laboratory or workspace.
- Do not eat or drink any substances tested unless expressly permitted to do so by a knowledgeable adult.

USING EQUIPMENT WITH CARE

- Set up apparatus far from the edge of the desk.
- Use knives or other sharp-pointed instruments with care.
- Pull plugs, not cords, when removing electrical plugs.
- Clean glassware before and after use.
- Check glassware for scratches, cracks, and sharp edges.
- Clean up broken glassware immediately.
- Do not use reflected sunlight to illuminate your microscope.
- Do not touch metal conductors.
- Use alcohol-filled thermometers, not mercury-filled thermometers.

USING CHEMICALS

- Never taste or inhale chemicals.
- Label all bottles and apparatus containing chemicals.
- Read labels carefully.
- Avoid chemical contact with skin and eyes (wear safety glasses, lab apron, and gloves).
- Do not touch chemical solutions.
- Wash hands before and after using solutions.
- Wipe up spills thoroughly.

HEATING SUBSTANCES

- Wear safety glasses, apron, and gloves when boiling water.
- Keep your face away from test tubes and beakers.
- Use test tubes, beakers, and other glassware made of Pyrex glass.
- Never leave apparatus unattended.
- Use safety tongs and heat-resistant gloves.

- If your laboratory does not have heat-proof workbenches, put your Bunsen burner on a heat-proof mat before lighting it.
- Take care when lighting your Bunsen burner; light it with the airhole closed, and use a Bunsen burner lighter in preference to wooden matches.
- Turn off hot plates, Bunsen burners, and gas when you are done.
- Keep flammable substances away from flames and other sources of heat.
- Have a fire extinguisher on hand.

FINISHING UP

- Thoroughly clean your work area and any glassware used.
- Wash your hands.
- Be careful not to return chemicals or contaminated reagents to the wrong containers.
- Do not dispose of materials in the sink unless instructed to do so.
- Clean up all residues and put them in proper containers for disposal.
- Dispose of all chemicals according to all local, state, and federal laws.

BE SAFETY CONSCIOUS AT ALL TIMES!

Science and the Origin of Art

When you hear the word *art*, what's the first thing that comes to mind? Maybe it's the *Mona Lisa* or some other famous painting. Perhaps it's a great statue or an ancient piece of decorated pottery. Yet, art is more than objects. Dance and music are also forms of art, as is poetry. In its most general sense, what we call art can include anything that is pleasing to the senses and has been created by a person or group of people. It is a form of expression that requires special skills and a great deal of imagination. In fact, the word *art* is taken from the Latin term *ars,* which means "skill."

Art also has a practical side. Because paintings and sculptures are pleasing to look at, they often are used to decorate spaces that would otherwise be plain and drab. **Artisans** are craftspeople who create useful objects, such as pottery, furniture, and tools. They often decorate their products to make them unique and more attractive. Art also comes into play in the design and construction of buildings and bridges. This is what **architecture** is all about.

On the surface, it may appear that the fields of art and science are opposites. Scientists are required to follow set procedures and methods, but artists are free to express themselves with few restrictions. There are some important similarities between the two fields though. Both scientists and artists need

The Taj Mahal in India exemplifies the role that art plays in construction. With its large, domed marble mausoleum to its symmetry, inlaid designs made with precious gems, and sprawling garden and reflecting pools, this visually stunning historical gem shows that buildings can be art.

to be careful observers of the world and must pay close attention to detail. They also need to be creative and use their imaginations to solve problems.

There is a great deal of science found in the arts. When a painter mixes colors on a palette, he or she must have a basic understanding about the physics of light. When a sculptor selects a stone from which to make a statue, he or she had better have an understanding of the basic geologic principles of hardness, fracture, and cleavage.

In this text, we will examine some of the science that lies at the heart of different forms of art. Because art is such a broad topic, we will focus primarily on the visual arts of drawing, painting, sculpture, and pottery. We also will look at the science behind architecture and discover how many of the same rules that govern art apply to the design and construction of buildings and bridges.

THE EARLIEST ARTISTS

It's impossible to know exactly when people first started creating works of art. Like language and music, art developed over a very long period of time. The first pieces of art probably were created by the same people who first learned to make tools from wood, bone, and stone. Scientists believe that the earliest forms of art are more than 40,000 years old. These were simple decorations carved or drawn on tools. Many of these decorations featured designs of animals that were hunted at the time. We can't know definitively why early artists carved these images, but it probably wasn't just to make things more attractive. By studying hunter/gatherer people who still live today, some scientists have interpreted these images as one way that a hunter could connect with the prey animal on a spiritual level.

Even today, many cultures will use pictures or sculptures of animals or people as "stand ins" for an actual living thing during a ritual. Perhaps these early hunters believed that putting an image of a bear on a spear would give them some type of power over the animal, making it easier for them to catch it. Because the first pieces of art were probably carved from wood or bone, a good place to begin our investigation into the science of art is to experience some wood carving firsthand. In **Experiment 1:** *Testing the Properties of Wood*, you will see how some of the properties of wood make it an ideal material to cut and carve.

EXPERIMENT 1
Testing the Properties of Wood

Topic

How do the properties of a piece of wood affect its ability to be carved?

Introduction

Wood was one of the materials used in early art. Because there are thousands of species of trees, wood has a wide range of properties that affect its ability to be shaped and carved. Even though ancient hunter/gatherers were technologically limited, they understood some of these properties. As a result, they selected different wood types for different uses. In this activity, you are going to test three types of wood to determine which properties are important for carving and shaping.

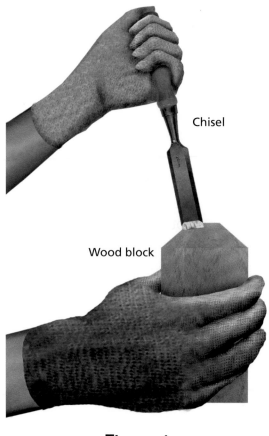

Chisel

Wood block

Figure 1

Time Required

60 minutes

Materials

- small wood chisel or flat blade screw driver
- small block of balsa wood (available at most hobby shops)
- small block of pine (available at most hobby shops)
- small block of maple or oak (available at most hobby shops)
- pair of heavy work gloves
- several pieces of fine sand paper (120 grit)
- adult to assist you

Safety Note During this experiment, you will be using a tool to carve a piece of wood. The tool will be sharp and could cause injury if not used properly. It is recommended that you conduct this activity under the supervision of a responsible adult.

Procedure

1. Examine the three pieces of wood. Pick up each piece and compare its weight. Use your thumbnail against the wood to test its hardness. Observe the grain of the wood and any other features that you might think are important. Record your observations.

2. Put on the gloves. Hold the piece of balsa wood in one hand. Using the chisel or screwdriver, carve the letter *T* into the block. Go slowly while using the tool so that it does not slip. Pay attention to the way the pieces of wood come off the block as you carve. Record your observations.

3. Repeat Step 2, using the block of pine and the block of oak or maple. Compare them to the balsa wood. Note any differences in the behavior of the wood as you are carving each block.

4. Remove the gloves, and slowly rub a finger over the edge of each block where you were carving it. Be careful not to get a splinter. Note the texture

of the wood. Rub the carved section of each block with the sandpaper to smooth the rough edges. Pay attention to the way the surface of the wood behaves, and record your observation.

Analysis

1. Which piece of wood appeared the hardest when you scratched it with your fingernail?

2. Which type of wood was easiest to carve?

3. How did the carved edge of the three pieces of wood change after they were rubbed with the sandpaper?

 ## What's Going On?

All wood comes from trees, but different types of trees produce wood with different properties. When it comes to carving wood to make sculptures or furniture, hardness is one of the most important properties. In general, softer wood is easier to carve, but there is a trade-off. Soft woods, such as balsa and pine, contain wood fibers that easily split when force is applied to them. When you dig into the wood with a carving tool, the fibers in softwood tend to peel off a surface. This makes it difficult to carve detailed features into the wood. In addition, when softwood is sanded, the fibers keep popping up, making it difficult to get a smooth finish.

Hardwoods such as oak, maple, and hickory are more difficult to carve. More force is needed to break the wood fibers. That means the carving tool needs to be sharper. Yet, because the fibers in hardwoods tend to break off in smaller pieces, an artist can create finer detail on the wood surface. When the surface of hardwood is sanded, it gets quite smooth.

Our Findings

Analysis

1. The maple or oak was much harder to scratch than either the balsa or pine.

2. The balsa was easiest to carve because it was quite soft.

3. After sanding, the maple or oak should have had a smooth texture, but the balsa was rough and "fuzzy." The pine was also smooth.

ROCK ON

Wood wasn't the only material that early artists carved. Other popular materials were ivory, bone, and stone. About 30,000 years ago, artists started carving images of people to go along with their animal sculptures. One common type of human-based sculpture is known as a Venus figure. These small statues usually were made of stone, and often showed a woman who appeared to be pregnant. Scientists and historians have different opinions about what these figures represented, but one popular idea is that they were fertility symbols. At the very least, the Venus figures show that artists were becoming quite accomplished at working with stone.

As with wood, there are many different types of rocks, each with its own properties. In **Experiment 2:** *Testing the Properties of Rocks*, you will determine which properties of a rock affect how it is sculpted.

EXPERIMENT 2
Testing the Properties of Rocks

Topic

Which properties of a rock affect its ability to be carved?

Introduction

Rocks have many properties, including color, crystal size and shape, density, and structure. Early artists discovered that some rocks were ideally suited for carving, whereas others were not. When it comes to shaping rocks, two important properties are hardness and cleavage. Hardness is a measure of how difficult a rock is to break or chip. Cleavage describes the way a rock breaks or fractures. It is controlled by the structure of the grains or crystals in a rock. In this activity, you are going to test three rock types to see how hardness and cleavage control a rock's ability to be shaped.

Stone chisel

Rock

Wooden block

Figure 1

Time Required

60 minutes

Materials

- chisel used for cutting rock or brick
- hammer
- steel nail
- magnifier
- piece of wood about 12 in. (30 cm) square and 2 in. (5 cm) thick
- fist-sized piece of limestone (available at building or garden supply stores)
- piece of slate approximately 6 in. (15 cm) square (available at building or gardening stores)
- fist-sized piece of granite (available at a building supply store or through monument dealers)
- heavy pair of work gloves
- goggles or safety glasses
- adult to assist you

Safety Note During this experiment, you will be using a tool to chip a piece of stone. You and anyone near you must wear safety glasses while doing this activity. Wear work gloves when striking the chisel with the hammer. Be careful not to hit your fingers. The tool will be sharp and could cause injury if not used properly. It is recommended that you conduct this activity under the supervision of a responsible adult.

Procedure

1. Feel the texture of the limestone. Use the magnifier to examine it closely, and describe how the particles that make up the rock join together. Scratch the surface of the rock with the point of the nail. Record your observations.
2. Repeat Step 1 with the slate and the granite samples.

3. Put on the gloves and goggles. Place the limestone onto the wooden board, and rest the point of the chisel on the surface of the rock. Strike the chisel with the hammer until the limestone breaks. Notice how much force it takes for you to break the limestone. Once you have removed a chip of rock, observe the broken edge. Record your observations.

4. Repeat Step 3, using the piece of slate and then the piece of granite. Compare these samples to the limestone. Note any differences in the way the three rocks break, and record your observations.

Analysis

1. Which rock sample appeared to be the hardest when you scratched it with the nail?

2. Which rock sample took the most effort to break?

3. How did the broken edge of the three samples of rock compare with one another?

 What's Going On?

The properties of a rock result from its formation. There are three main ways in which rock is formed. Granite is an igneous rock. It forms under Earth's surface as magma (liquid rock) cools and crystallizes. Granite usually has large interlocking crystals. It is quite hard and difficult to break. Limestone is a sedimentary rock. It forms from the recombination of weathered pieces of other rocks (called sediment). In most limestone, the individual grains are quite small. Limestone is much softer than granite and usually breaks with a smoother edge. Slate is a metamorphic rock. It forms when other rocks are heated and squeezed. The heat and high pressure cause mineral crystals to realign within the rock. As a result, when a slate is hit, it generally cleaves, or breaks, along the aligned crystals, leaving a jagged edge.

Both limestone and granite are used for sculptures. Because limestone is softer, it is easier to shape and create fine details. Carving granite requires more time and effort, but the resulting sculpture is more resistant to wear and damage from the elements. Granite sculptures are ideally suited for outdoor use. This is why many of the monuments and tombstones found in cemeteries are made from granite. When left outdoors, carvings made from limestone are quickly worn down by rain and wind. Because slate often breaks in long parallel sheets, it is difficult to carve into sculptures. It is, however, an ideal material for paving walkways.

Our Findings

1. The granite sample was the most difficult to scratch.
2. The granite was the most difficult rock to break.
3. Because it is made of fine grains, the limestone usually leaves a relatively smooth edge. The granite should have had a rough edge, and the slate should have broken in layers.

MODERN STONE WORK

Over the years, the tools used by stone carvers have changed, but many artists' techniques developed thousands of years ago are still in use today. The first step in making a sculpture is selecting the proper stone. Just about any rock can be shaped into a sculpture, but most stone carvers focus on five types (from softest to hardest): soapstone, alabaster, limestone, marble, and granite.

Once a stone has been selected, the artist will "rough out" a design by using a mallet and a large chisel to chip off pieces. Most often, the chisel will look like a large spike with a pointed tip. However, if an artist needs to remove a large amount of stone, he might use a pitching tool. This tool has a large, flat blade that is ideal for splitting off large pieces of rock. After the basic shape is completed, the artist will use smaller, specialized chisels to refine the piece. In the final stages of carving, artists change from chipping to rubbing. Abrasive tools include rasps and rifflers, which look like files. These tools remove the chisel marks and smooth the surface of the stone.

An artist can easily add or remove material when working with clay. This provides an advantage over working with other materials, such as stone and wood.

The final two steps involve sanding and polishing the piece. Sanding stone is like sanding a piece of wood, except that the grit on the sandpaper is much harder. The sandpaper used on stone is usually made from tiny particles of silicon carbide, which is much harder than normal sand. When sanding granite and other hard stones, some artists will use paper with tiny diamonds embedded in it. For the final polishing, a sculptor will use a fine grit called rouge, as well as a buffing wheel or cloth. The entire process requires a great deal of effort. It can take months to complete one sculpture. In the end, though, a statue made from stone will stand the test of time. After all, museums all over the world are filled with stone statues that are thousands of years old.

MOLDING CLAY

Nature provides art materials other than stone. One of the most important art-related discoveries was **clay**. Clay is a type of **sediment** formed from rocks that have been worn away over time. Working with clay offers several advantages over stone or wood. Both stone and wood are hard and are shaped by chipping pieces away. This is a *destructive* process. Working with clay is a *constructive* process. A clay sculpture is built from smaller pieces added together. When carving stone, if an artist chips away too much rock, there is no way to put it back. With clay, you can add or remove material at any time during the sculpting process. In **Experiment 3:** *Testing the Properties of Sediment*, you will examine some of the other unique properties of clay that make it an ideal medium for sculptures and pottery.

EXPERIMENT 3
Testing the Properties of Sediment

Topic

What properties of sediment allow it to be molded into shapes?

Introduction

Gravel, sand, and clay are different types of sediment. They are formed from worn and weathered pieces of rock. The main difference between these three

Figure 1

sediment types is their size. By definition, rock particles larger than 0.0788 in. (2 mm) in diameter are considered to be gravel. Sand-sized grains are between 0.0788 in. and 0.00197 in. (2.0 mm and 0.05 mm, respectively) in diameter. Clay grains are the smallest. To be considered clay, a particle has to be smaller than 0.0000788 in. (0.0002 mm) in diameter. Unlike sand and gravel, individual clay grains are so small that they cannot be seen, even with a high-powered light microscope. In this experiment, you will compare some of the different properties of sand and clay and test to see how clay can be separated from other types of sediment. In addition, you will discover which properties of clay make it an ideal material for molding into sculptures and pottery.

Time Required

This activity should be conducted over a two-day period. It will require 45 minutes the first day and 15 minutes the second day.

Materials

- 1 cup (250 ml) dry natural modeling clay, available at an art supply store
- 1 cup (250 ml) dry fine sand, available at a building supply store
- graduated cylinder or measuring cup
- empty clear plastic 1-liter soda bottle with cap, remove the label
- 2 small plastic bowls
- 2 plastic spoons
- paper towels
- magnifier
- watch or timer
- water

Safety Note No special safety precautions are needed for this activity. Please review and follow the safety guidelines before proceeding.

Procedure

1. Pour the dry samples of sand and clay into two separate plastic bowls. Use the magnifier to examine each sample closely. Pinch a small amount of each sample between your thumb and forefinger and rub it back and forth a few times. Describe how each sample looks and feels. Record your observations.

2. Pour ¼ cup (about 50 ml) of water into each bowl. Mix each bowl of sediment and water with a spoon. After mixing, pinch a small amount of each mixture between your thumb and forefinger and rub it back and forth. After testing each sample, return the sediment mixture to the proper bowl and wipe off your fingers with a damp paper towel. Record your observations.

3. Put about half of the wet clay into the plastic soda bottle. Put half of the sand sample in the same bottle as the clay. Fill the bottle about ¾ full with water, and screw on the cap. Shake the bottle vigorously for about 10 seconds and then place it on a table. Observe what happens to the sediment in the bottle as it stands. Allow the bottle to rest undisturbed on the table for 15 minutes. Continue with Step 4 while you are waiting.

4. Squeeze the remaining clay in your hand. Observe what happens when you try to roll it into a ball. Place the clay back in the bowl and repeat the procedure with the remaining sand. Describe and record how each type of sediment behaves when you squeeze and roll it. Place the two bowls in a safe place and allow them to sit undisturbed for about 24 hours to dry out.

5. Return to the soda bottle and look at the sediment. Record your observations.

6. After waiting 24 hours, examine the sand and clay samples in the bowls. Hold each in your hand and describe how they feel. Record your observations.

Analysis

1. How did the two sediment samples feel when they were dry?
2. How did the two sediment samples feel when they were wet?
3. What happened to the wet samples when you squeezed them in your hand?
4. What happened to the sediment after you mixed it with water in the soda bottle and allowed it to stand for 15 minutes?
5. How did the sand compare to the clay after you allowed the samples to dry for 24 hours?

What's Going On?

Scientists and historians aren't certain when people first started making objects from clay, but evidence from archeological sites in the Middle East and China suggest that it has been done for at least 9,000 years. Unlike sand, which is a coarse-grained sediment, clay particles are extremely fine. When clay is wet, it is **plastic**. It can be molded into almost any shape, and will stay that way. By contrast, sand is difficult to mold, even when wet. When clay dries, it hardens and resembles stone. This means that a sculpture or bowl made from clay will keep its shape unless it gets wet again. When sand dries, the grains separate.

All sediment is the result of the weathering and erosion of rock. Running water in rivers and streams picks up and transports sediment downstream. In a standing body of water, such as a pond or lake, the flowing water loses its ability to carry the sediment. As a result, the sediment begins to settle to the bottom. Because sand particles are larger and heavier, they tend to settle quickly, while clay grains stay suspended in the water for a longer period of time. This process helps to naturally separate types of sediment by size. It often creates layers of pure clay on the bottom of a pond or lake. Over time, ponds and lakes fill with sediment and dry out, leaving clay deposits behind. People discovered that they could dig up clay and use it for pottery, sculptures, and even building materials, such as bricks and tiles.

Our Findings

1. The clay felt smooth and powdery, but the sand was rough and gritty.
2. The clay felt slick and sticky, but the sand was damp and rough.
3. When damp clay is squeezed, it forms a tight ball. The wet sand held together only slightly.
4. When the two sediment types were placed in the bottle with water and shaken, they mixed. When the bottle was allowed to stand, the sand quickly settled to the bottom, and the clay stayed in suspension. After 15 minutes, two distinct layers formed with the sand on the bottom and the clay on top.
5. After drying for 24 hours, the clay ball was hard, and the sand returned to being loose grains.

CERAMICS IN THE MODERN WORLD

Ceramics is not only a popular art form, but also a big business. The word *ceramic* comes from the Greek *keramos* which means "clay." Ceramics include a wide range of items—everything from simple flower pots to fine china. In addition to being pleasant-looking, many ceramic objects, such as cups, plates, tiles, and a wide range of pottery, also serve a useful purpose.

Many of the techniques used by potters today have their origins in the ancient world. Perhaps the most important discovery was the firing of clay objects. Firing is the process by which clay is hardened and chemically changed at a high temperature. The firing of clay was probably an accidental discovery. More than likely, someone discovered that a clay vessel that had been placed in a fire became harder and more water resistant. Early potters fired their works by placing them in a fire. Somewhere around 6,000 B.C., people discovered that a better approach was to bake the clay in an oven. This idea led to the development of the first **kiln**.

Another discovery that helped make ceramics more durable was the process of glazing. Glaze is a type of glass that forms

A kiln is an oven used for baking clay to create ceramics. Heat causes hardening and chemical changes to the clay, making it more durable.

on the outside of the clay that has been heated to high temperatures. Glazing compounds are made from a wide variety of materials. When they are heated, they melt and fuse together. Glazing gives the outside of the ceramic a shiny appearance. In addition, the glaze will usually waterproof the clay. This comes in handy for items such as cups, bowls, and jugs.

One final development that helped to revolutionize the making of ceramics was the invention of the potter's wheel. This device dates back to around 4000 B.C. The first wheels were simple turntables made from wood. They rotated horizontally on an axis. As the wheel spins, an artist can place a hand or tool against the side of the clay and shape it. The rotation allows the shape of the object to be much more symmetrical. In addition, by punching a hole in the top of the clay and holding a hand inside, a potter can move the clay upward, making a vessel with thin sides.

MAKING THE MOST OF METALS

Of all the artistic artifacts that can be viewed at museums today, the most spectacular often are made of metal. Pieces made from gold, silver, and copper show levels of detail not possible with clay or stone. About 10,000 years ago, copper became the first metal used for artistic purposes.

Metals, such as copper, silver, and gold, often can be found as pure nuggets or lumps lying on the ground along streams. In this form, they are called native elements. Most other metals, including iron, zinc, aluminum, and tin, are almost always

This red hot iron is being hammered into shape on top of an anvil. Heating the metal makes it more malleable.

 **Materials**

- regular hammer
- sledgehammer
- sturdy table
- phone book
- 3 pieces of thick steel wire, each about 6 in. (15 cm) long (these can be cut from a metal coat hanger)
- 3 wooden popsicle sticks or tongue depressors
- small piece of fine (120 grit) sandpaper
- heavy pair of work gloves
- goggles or safety glasses
- adult to assist you

Safety Note During this experiment, you will be using a hammer to strike several different objects. You and anyone near you should wear safety glasses while doing this activity. When striking the objects with the hammer, you should wear work gloves. Be careful not to hit your fingers. It is recommended that you conduct this activity under the supervision of a responsible adult.

Procedure

1. Carefully examine the metal wire and the wooden sticks. Compare the texture and hardness of each material, and record your observations.
2. Put on the gloves and goggles. Hold one end of the wooden stick in each hand, and slowly bend the two ends of the stick toward each other until they touch. Observe what happens. Repeat the same procedure, using the metal wire. Record your results.
3. Place the telephone book on a sturdy table. Place the head of the sledge-hammer on top of the book, as in Figure 1. In this part of the activity, the sledgehammer will act like an anvil on which you will rest the different materials. Have an adult hold the handle of the sledgehammer so that it doesn't move. Grasp one end of the second wooden stick in one hand, and place the other end on top of the sledgehammer. Hit the end of the

stick several times with the smaller hammer. Observe what happens. Repeat the procedure with the second piece of metal wire. Record your observations.

4. Hold one end of the third wooden stick firmly. Sand the other end several times and observe what happens to surface of the stick. Repeat the procedure with the third metal wire. Record your observations.

Analysis

1. What happened to the wooden stick when you tried to touch the two ends together? How did this compare with the metal wire?

2. What happened to the end of the wooden stick when you hit it with the hammer? How did this compare to the metal wire?

3. What happened to the wooden stick when you rubbed it with the sandpaper? How did this compare to the metal wire?

 ## What's Going On?

When stone or wood is subjected to stress, it tends to split and break. Though these materials are hard, they are also brittle. Most natural metals are considered **ductile**. When subjected to stress, they bend. Many metals also are malleable. They can be flattened into a thin sheet. This unique property allows metals such as gold and silver to be shaped into intricate patterns with fine details.

A metal's surface is usually shiny when polished. This is why metals such as gold and silver are used for ornaments and jewelry.

Our Findings

1. The wooden stick snapped, whereas the metal wire bent.

2. The end of wooden stick splintered when it was hit it, whereas the end of the metal wire flattened out.

3. The surface of the wooden stick became smoother when sanded, whereas the surface of the metal wire began to shine.

MODERN METALLURGY

Metal wasn't used only for artistic and decorative purposes. People realized that because of its unique properties, metals such as copper could be turned into tools and weapons. Over time, people developed techniques that improved the quality and performance of metal items. One of the first improvements was the act of annealing, which is a process that involves periodically heating a piece of metal in a fire before hammering it. Annealing helps to relieve the internal stresses in a piece of metal, making it less likely to crack when it is being shaped.

The idea of heating metals soon led to the process of smelting. As noted earlier, most metals do not occur as native elements. Instead, they are found in ores, combined with other minerals in rocks. In order for the metal to be used, it must first be separated from the other minerals. The first smelting of copper from ore happened about 6,000 years ago. It was made possible by the invention of the two-chamber pottery kiln. This special oven allowed artisans to heat pottery to much higher temperatures, creating better glazes. More than likely, some rocks containing copper were placed in the kiln along with the pots, and the result was a piece of pure copper.

The ability to heat metal to higher temperatures led to the production of **alloys**. Alloys are metals made by mixing two or more metals—or a metal with another substance—in a molten (melted) state. Making alloys allowed people to create new metals with different properties. One of the first alloys was bronze, a combination of copper and tin. Bronze is harder than pure copper, and it holds a much sharper edge, making it better suited for swords and knives. Today, most of the metals we use are alloys. The gold found in rings, for example, is not pure. It is usually an alloy of gold and either silver or platinum. This makes a ring harder and less likely to bend. One of the most important alloys to come from the working of metal is steel, an alloy of iron and carbon. As we will discover later, if it were not for the development of steel, most modern architecture would be impossible.

DRAWING PICTURES AND PAINTING WITH COLORS

So far the discussion of the origins of art has focused on the techniques and materials used in the making of sculptures, pottery, and jewelry. Three dimensional objects weren't the only forms of art. The first evidence of people drawing and painting on rocks and inside caves comes from about 20,000 years ago.

People have been creating art for centuries, as demonstrated by early rock and cave drawings that people made with natural pigments. These bison drawings were found in a cave in Altamira, Spain.

Some of the earliest attempts at drawing used charcoal, produced by burning the end of a stick. In addition, people made handprints using mud and ashes mixed with water.

Probably the most famous of these early drawings can be found inside caves in Lascaux, France, and Altamira, Spain. It was in those locations that scientists discovered the skilled drawings of horses, bison, deer, and other animals hunted at that time in history. What's even more impressive is that the artists colored the pictures using natural **pigments**, or materials in paint that provide color. In **Experiment 5:** *Creating Primitive Pigments*, you will experiment with making your own simple paints using some basic ingredients that might be found in any kitchen.

EXPERIMENT 5

Creating Primitive Pigments

Topic

How did people of the past create simple paints using natural ingredients?

Introduction

Paints are applied to the surface of an object to change its color or design. In the hands of a talented artist, paints can be used to create masterpieces, and in the hands of a homeowner, they can be used to change the color of a room. In addition to their decorative value, paints are also used to protect surfaces from weather. Steel bridges are painted to keep the metal from corroding. Wooden buildings are painted to keep them from rotting. Paints are liquid when they are applied. Once exposed to the air, paint begins to dry, forming a solid layer on the outer surface of an object.

The first known use of paints dates back to about 20,000 years ago, when ancient artists used natural pigments to create cave paintings showing hunting scenes. In this activity, you will use a fruit extract as a pigment and develop a simple paint formula.

Time Required

60 minutes

Materials:

- 1 cup (250 ml) ripe fresh or frozen (thawed) blueberries
- ¼ stick butter, room temperature
- 1 egg
- small mixing bowl
- tea strainer or large slotted spoon
- metal fork
- metal teaspoon

- 3 disposable plastic cups
- water
- small artist's paintbrush
- 3 pieces white bond or copier paper
- paper towels

Safety Note No special safety precautions are needed for this activity. Please review and follow the safety guidelines before proceeding.

Procedure

1. With a fork, mash the blueberries in the mixing bowl. Break up the skins as much as possible. The berries should look like a thick paste when you are done.

2. Place the strainer over one of the plastic cups. Pour about one-third of the mashed blueberries into the strainer. Use the back of the metal spoon to

Figure 1

push the berry juice through the strainer and into the cup. (See Figure 1). The blueberry skins should remain in the strainer. Empty the strainer and repeat the procedure, placing the rest of the mashed berries into the second and third cup. When you are finished, wash the strainer and the bowl so that the blueberries do not stain them.

3. Add the butter to one of the cups of blueberry extract. Use the fork to mix the butter in with the blueberry juice until the mixture resembles a thick paste. When you are finished, wash the fork. Carefully crack the egg with the fork and allow the egg white to drain into the second cup. Try not to get any of the yolk in the cup. Use the fork to mix the egg white with the blueberry juice. Do not add anything to the third cup of blueberry extract.

4. Label one piece of paper "berries only," another piece "berries with butter," and the third piece "berries with egg white." Dip the paintbrush into the plain berry extract and make a large spot on the paper labeled "berries only." Clean off the brush with a damp paper towel, and repeat the procedure using the other two mixtures and pieces of paper. Clean the brush with warm soapy water as soon as you have finished.

5. Allow the painted paper to dry for 45 minutes. Observe the three painted spots.

Analysis

1. What was the color of the blueberry juice after you pushed it through the strainer?

2. How did the juice mixed with butter and the juice mixed with egg white compare with the plain extract?

3. When you painted the spots on the paper, which extract produced the darkest color?

4. How did the three painted spots compare after they were allowed to stand for 45 minutes?

 What's Going On?

If you have ever spilled grape juice or ketchup on your shirt, you know that many natural materials contain pigments that can permanently change the color of your clothes. Pigments mixed with water do not make good paints, however, because they fade quickly. In order to be an effective paint, a pigment must be mixed with another liquid that serves as a binder. When the binder dries, the pigment remains fixed and the paint keeps its color.

The first paints were made from mineral pigments, such as iron oxide (rust), which were found in rocks and ground into powder. The pigment was then mixed with substances, such as animal fat, natural glue from plants and fish, and even blood. By about 4000 B.C., Egyptian artists discovered that a rich pigment could be extracted from the indigo plant. When mixed with egg white, the pigment made a fine paint. Eventually, people discovered that certain oils would serve as better binders than egg white. Oil paint is extremely effective, but has a terrible odor until it fully dries, sometimes taking several days. Oil-based paints are still in use today, but they have largely been replaced by latex paint, which is made from synthetic rubber. First used in 1949, latex paints look almost as good as oil-based paints but offer several advantages: They dry in only a few hours, can be cleaned up with soap and water, and have less odor.

Our Findings

1. The blueberry juice was a purplish color.
2. The juice mixed with butter was thicker than the juice mixed with egg white. The plain juice was the thinnest.
3. The extract mixed with the butter produced the darkest color.
4. After 45 minutes, the plain juice on the paper faded. The juice mixed with butter remained dark purple and was wet to the touch. The juice mixed with the egg white dried and was darker than the plain juice but not quite as dark as the juice mixed with butter.

FRESCOS, CANVAS, AND PAPER

As artists became more skilled at creating and using pigments, they also began experimenting with painting on different surfaces, such as wood and dried animal skins. One major use of paint was to decorate pottery. Many examples dating back more than 5,000 years can be found in Egyptian tombs and on the island of Crete. About this same time, we see the first examples of **frescos**. *Fresco* is based on the Italian word meaning "fresh"; it is a type of painting in which paint is applied directly to plaster that is still wet, or fresh. Frescos can be found on the walls of many ancient buildings and tombs. They are well preserved, partly because of the way the paint is applied. As the wet plaster dries, the paint in a fresco becomes part of the wall surface.

In Europe, frescos reached their peak during the Renaissance period in the late 1400s and early 1500s. It was then that masters, such as Leonardo da Vinci, Raphael, and Michelangelo, created some of their most notable works. Michelangelo created an impressive fresco on the ceiling of the Sistine Chapel in Rome. It took him four years to finish it. Visitors in modern times are typically awestruck by the detail and beauty of the colors frozen in time.

Walls and ceilings weren't the only things that Renaissance artists were painting. For portraits and landscapes, artists were using oil paints on **canvas**. Canvas is a tightly woven, heavy cloth. It was originally used to make tents, sails, and packs. Before canvas, artists had painted on linen stretched over wooden boards. Because linen is lightweight fabric with spaces between the threads, paints would soak in and run together. Canvas is heavy enough to stretch over a wooden frame and does not need any backing. Because the weave of canvas is so tight, paint rests on top rather than soaking in deeply.

Many modern artists still use canvas, but before they paint, they typically sketch an idea on a piece of paper. The earliest artists did not have this option: paper is a relatively recent invention. The first paperlike material was developed in Egypt around 3000 B.C., when scribes first learned to make papyrus reed scrolls. The first true paper was developed much later in China. In **Experiment 6: *Making Paper***, you will try to make paper—and discover the process that an enterprising individual named Cai Lun came up with almost 2,000 years ago.

Making Paper

Topic

How is paper made?

Introduction

The origins of modern papermaking can be traced to China. Before the invention of paper, scribes in China wrote on scrolls made from either bamboo or silk. Both of these materials proved difficult to work with, and people experimented with other fibers. According to the most popular legend, in A.D. 105, Chinese scribe Cai Lun came up with a workable formula. First, he mixed ground up tree bark, old hemp fishnets, and shredded bamboo in a pot of water. He pounded the mixture into a thick pulp and spread it on a screen. After the mixture dried, he was able to peel it off the screen, and the result was a light weight material that could be used for writing, drawing, and painting. In this activity, you are going to replicate some of Cai Lun's original papermaking process in order to find out what holds a piece of paper together.

Time Required

This activity will require 60 minutes on the first day. After 24 hours, you will need an additional 5 minutes to examine the results of the experiment.

Materials

- roll of paper towels (plain white works best)
- large mixing bowl
- measuring cup
- water
- 2 pieces of window screen, 6 in. x 12 in. (15 cm x 30 cm)
- eggbeater or hand mixer
- small mixing bowl

- rolling pin

- magnifier

- sturdy table or countertop that can get wet

- old towel or large cloth rag

- adult to assist you

> **Safety Note** **No special safety precautions are needed for this activity. Please review and follow the safety guidelines before proceeding.**

Procedure

1. Rip off a paper towel sheet from the roll and examine it closely with the magnifier. Tear the sheet in half and observe the torn edge. Tear the paper towel into little bits and place the pieces into the mixing bowl. Shred two more sheets of paper the same way and add them to the bowl.

2. Pour 2 cups (500 ml) of water into the bowl and mix the paper pieces and water thoroughly with your hand. Allow the paper to soak for about 10 minutes. Mix the paper and water with the eggbeater or hand mixer. Blend for one minute. Pick up a handful of the mixture. Observe its texture and note any changes to it as compared to what you saw in Step 1.

3. Spread the towel or rag on a table or similar sturdy surface. Dip one of the screens into the bowl so that the paper/water mixture flows over it. Lift the screen out of the bowl and pull the two sides tight so that it is horizontal. The screen should be directly over the bowl, so that any water dripping through the screen goes back into the bowl. Have your assistant smooth the wet paper mixture over the top of the screen. Make sure that the screen in evenly covered with the mixture. If need be, have your assistant reach into the bowl to get extra mixture to fill in any bare spots. Allow the water to drip through the screen for about one minute, and then lay the screen flat on the towel or rag.

4. Place the second screen directly on top of the first screen. The paper mixture should be sandwiched in between the screens. Press down on the top screen with the rolling pin. Roll the rolling pin forward slowly, pushing the water out as you go. Roll back and forth across the screen until you have squeezed out most of the water. Tap gently on the top screen a few times with your fingertips so that it separates from the paper below. Remove

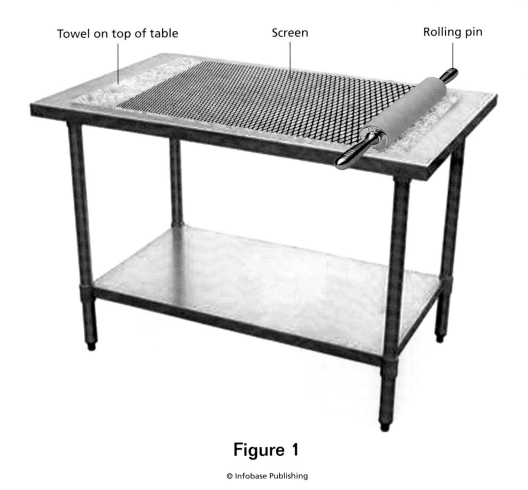

Towel on top of table   Screen   Rolling pin

Figure 1

© Infobase Publishing

the top screen and allow the paper mixture on the lower screen to dry for about 30 minutes.

5. After the paper has dried, pick up the screen by the edges and flip it over on the table. Tap on the screen until the paper falls off. Allow the paper to dry overnight. The next day, pick it up and examine it. Compare it with a fresh paper towel from the roll.

Analysis

1. What did the torn edge of the paper towel look like under the magnifier?

2. What happened to the torn pieces of paper towel after they soaked in the water for 10 minutes?

3. What did the paper/water mixture feel like after you mixed it with the eggbeater?

4. After the paper on the screen dried, how did its texture compare with that of the fresh sheet of paper towel from the roll?

What's Going On?

Today, paper comes in many different types and grades; among them are bond paper, copier paper, newspaper, construction paper, craft paper, paper towels, and even toilet paper. Each type of paper has its own unique properties, but all paper is made basically the same way. Most paper is made from cellulose fibers. Cellulose is a natural polymer that makes up the cell walls of plants. If you tear a piece of paper and look at the rough edge with a magnifier, you can see these fibers. They look like little hairs.

The first step in papermaking is breaking and separating the cellulose fibers. This step is done by shredding or grinding the plant material and mixing it with water. The result is a thick liquid suspension called pulp. The pulp is then spread over a screen and squeezed under high pressure to remove most of the water. In this step, the fibers get compressed to make a single sheet. After the rest of the water evaporates, the paper can be removed and put to use.

In order to make different types of paper, manufacturers will mix different types of fibers. In some cases, they will use fabric threads and even synthetic materials. In addition to different fibers, manufacturers will also add materials such as clay, bleach, and colored dyes to give the final product an even wider range of properties.

Our Findings

1. The edge of the torn paper was fuzzy with little fibers sticking out of it.
2. After the torn pieces of paper soaked in the water, they began to separate.
3. After the paper and water mixture was beaten, it was very mushy and soft.
4. Results will vary, but the paper from the screen was probably a little thicker than a paper towel and it had uneven patches on the surface.

PAINTBRUSHES AND PENCILS

Before we end this section on the origins of art, let's look at the history of some of the tools that artists use to draw and paint. One of the first implements developed was the paintbrush. Brushes are simple to make. All you need to do is collect a bunch of fibers, bind them together, and add a handle. Many of the early cave paintings in Altamira, Spain, were done using brushes, as were tomb paintings done by the Egyptians. Before the invention of the brush, artists might have used their fingers to apply liquid paint, or they might have ground solid pigment and blown it onto a sticky surface using a hollow bone or piece of wood. As you might expect, these methods didn't allow an artist to create many details. By changing the size and shape of the paintbrush fibers that were used, people could make brushes for a variety of different jobs—from painting broad strokes to making fine lines.

At first, artists probably made brushes from plant fibers. Then, soon enough, someone discovered that a better quality brush could be made from animal hair. One of the most popular types of hair was hog bristles. Hog's hair is ideal for use in paintbrushes because the bottom end of a hair is thick and broad, and the top end splits into a series of small filaments. Hog's hair is tough, so it stands up to repeated use and can hold paint. Today, paintbrushes are often made from synthetic fibers, such as nylon, but many artists still prefer to use natural hog's hair brushes to do their work.

Unlike the paintbrush, the pencil is a much more recent invention. A pencil has a solid core of soft material called lead, which is surrounded by a wooden or metal tube. In 1565 German naturalist Conrad Gesner was the first person to describe how to make a pencil. Before pencils, artists would use charcoal to sketch their drawings. Charcoal as a drawing tool dates back to prehistoric times, and it is still used by artists today. However, charcoal smears easily, and it is difficult to make clear, sharp lines using it. The pencil solves both of these problems.

A common lead pencil contains no lead at all. The black material is made from the mineral graphite. Originally, graphite was thought to be a type of lead, which is why the center core is called lead. Graphite is actually a type of pure carbon, similar to charcoal. As a pencil is dragged over a drawing surface, **friction** wears off some of the graphite. Pencil lead is made by mixing graphite with clay. The more clay in the mix, the harder the pencil lead is.

Light and Color

Whether it is a marble statue, a fine oil painting, or a simple black and white photograph, the way the light behaves when it hits a piece of artwork is critical. Not only does light control the shading and clarity of the image, but it is also responsible for the colors. Before we can truly understand the way that artists use light, we must first take a look at the physics of light.

LIGHT AND DARK

Light is a form of energy. Energy is what makes things move or change. In order for you to see something, light energy traveling from an object has to hit your eye and stimulate the cells of your retina, which is at the back of your eye. From there, the energy is carried by the optic nerve to your brain, which creates the image of the object. In the space between an object and your eye, many things can happen to light—and all of them can change the way an object appears to you. In **Experiment 7: Making Shadows,** you'll discover how blocking a source of light can create some unusual visual effects.

Making Shadows

Topic

How are shadows created and changed?

Introduction

When light leaves a source—such as the Sun, a distant star, or even a light bulb—it moves out in a series of straight paths called rays. When a number of rays all travel in the same direction, they make a **beam**. If you turn on a flashlight and shine it across a dark room, you will produce a beam of light. The beam will travel in the same direction in which you point the flashlight. When a beam of light strikes an object, the path of the individual light rays are changed. In this experiment, you will discover what happens when a beam of light is partially blocked.

Time Required

30 minutes

Materials

- bright flashlight
- sheet of white copier paper
- masking tape
- table or counter next to a wall in a room that can be made dark
- pencil
- thick book
- small ball of modeling clay
- yardstick or meterstick

Procedure

1. Stick the paper to the wall with masking tape, directly above the top of the table or counter. The paper will serve as a screen. Make the room as dark as possible. Turn on the flashlight and rest it on the thick book. Place the book on the table so that the lens of the light is about 24 in. (60 cm) from the wall. The light should be pointed directly at the white paper, and you should see a white spot on the paper. Slowly slide the book closer to the paper and observe the spot. Then slowly pull the book back from the paper until it is at the far end of the table. Observe the spot as you move the flashlight and book back and forth a few times.

2. Set the flashlight and book in their original position, 24 in. (60 cm) from the paper. Push the pointed end of the pencil into the lump of clay. The pencil should be able to stand on its own. Place the pencil 12 in. (30 cm) from the wall between the front of the flashlight and the paper. Observe the image on the white paper.

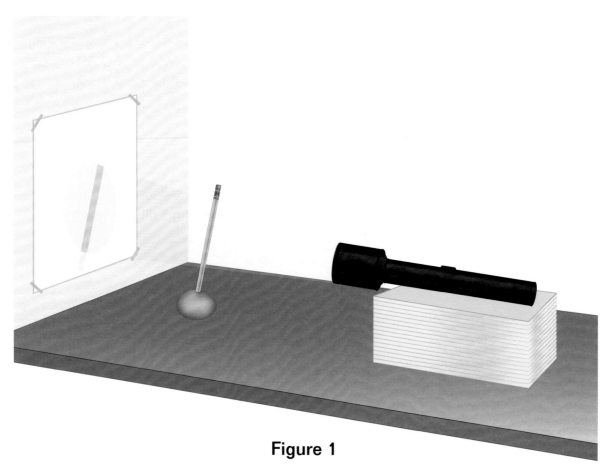

Figure 1

3. Slowly move the pencil forward until it is about 6 in. (15 cm) from the wall. Observe what happens to the image on the white paper. Move the pencil toward the flashlight until it is 18 in. (45 cm) from the wall. Observe what happens to the image on the paper.

4. Place the pencil 6 in. (15 cm) from the wall. Start with the flashlight 24 in. (60 cm) from the wall. Slowly move the flashlight closer to the wall until it is directly behind the pencil. Observe what you see on the white paper as you move the light forward.

Analysis

1. What happened to the spot on the paper as you moved the flashlight closer and farther from the screen?

2. What did you observe on the white paper when you placed the pencil in front of the flashlight?

3. What happened to the shadow created by the pencil as you moved it closer and farther from the wall?

4. What happened to the shadow created by the pencil as you moved the flashlight closer to the pencil?

 What's Going On?

Because the individual light rays that make up a beam of light are not exactly parallel to each other, a beam of light will begin to spread as it moves from its source. When an object is placed in front of a light beam, it blocks some of the rays. This creates a shadow. Shadows often have two parts: an inner darker part called the umbra and a less distinct outer part called the penumbra. The umbra is darker because the object blocks all of the rays of light from getting behind it. The penumbra forms when only some of the rays are blocked; others get by and fill in the gap.

The size and clarity of a shadow depend on several factors, including the size of the object and the size and brightness of the light source. Other factors include the distance between the light source and the object and the distance between the object and the surface on which the shadow falls. If a light source is far away from an object, and the light source is large and bright like the Sun, then the shadow cast behind the object will be fairly sharp and well defined. That's because the object is blocking most of the rays of light that are hitting it. The shadow has only an umbra. If a large bright light source is brought near an object, the shadow will be fuzzy because many of the light rays striking it bend around the object and fill in behind it. This causes a penumbra to form.

When they design their works, artists and architects consider how light will create shadows. Sculptors will often set the lines and curves of their pieces to create shadows on some parts and highlights on others. Architects may design buildings to work with the daily and seasonal positions of the Sun. By setting overhangs and roof lines at precise angles, they can let sunlight shine on certain parts of the building while sheltering other parts. This is particularly important when it comes to the design of passive solar buildings, which depend heavily on sunlight for heating and cooling.

Our Findings

1. As the flashlight moved closer to the screen, the spot of light became smaller and brighter.

2. When the pencil was moved in front of the flashlight, it cast a shadow on the paper behind it.

3. When the pencil moved closer to the light, the shadow became larger and less defined (fuzzier). When the pencil moved closer to the wall, the shadow became smaller and its edges became sharper.

4. When the light moved closer to the pencil, the shadow became larger and less defined.

HOW LIGHT PRODUCES COLOR

One of the most important parts of any piece of artwork—or of a room, for that matter—is the color scheme. Even a slight color change can have a major impact. Even though it may seem as if objects have color in them, the truth is that the colors we see come from light striking the object. If you take an apple that looks bright red in sunlight and put it in a dimly lit room, the color fades. If you take that same red apple and shine a single blue spotlight on it, the apple will look black. To understand how light produces color, we must first look at how light travels.

As we said at the beginning of this section, light is a form of energy. It is known as electromagnetic radiation. It travels in a series of pulses called **electromagnetic waves** created at the source of the light when electrons begin vibrating. Electromagnetic radiation comes in many forms. Along with the light we see (called visible light) there are radio waves, microwaves, infrared radiation (heat), ultra violet rays, x-rays, and gamma rays. Each type of radiation has a different **frequency** and **wavelength**. Frequency is defined as the number of times a wave vibrates in a second. Wavelength is the distance between one wave and the next. Taken as a group, these different types of

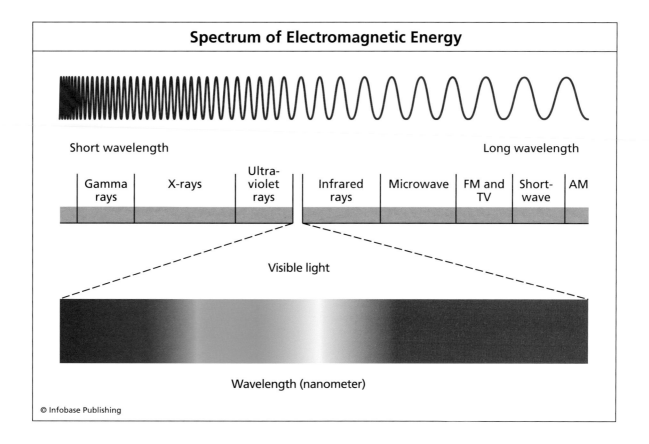

Spectrum of Electromagnetic Energy

Short wavelength   Long wavelength

| Gamma rays | X-rays | Ultra-violet rays | Infrared rays | Microwave | FM and TV | Short-wave | AM |

Visible light

Wavelength (nanometer)

© Infobase Publishing

electromagnetic radiation make a broad band of energy called the **electromagnetic spectrum.**

Within the electromagnetic spectrum, radio waves have the longest wavelength and vibrate with the lowest frequency. At the other end of the spectrum are gamma rays. These have extremely short wavelengths and high frequencies. Visible light waves are near the middle. Using specialized equipment, it is possible to separate electromagnetic waves of different frequencies. When it comes to the visible light part of the spectrum, this separation allows us to produce different colors of light. In **Experiment 8:** *Separating and Blending Colors of Light,* you will create colors by separating and blending different frequencies of light.

EXPERIMENT
8

Separating and Blending Colors of Light

Topic

How can colors of light be separated and blended?

Introduction

If you look at a beam of light coming from a flashlight or the Sun, it appears to be white. In the 1600s, Sir Isaac Newton discovered that white light is really made of several colors. Using a triangular piece of glass called a prism, Newton was able to separate white light into its component colors. Using a second prism, he recombined the individual colors to make white light again. In this activity, you will recreate Newton's experiment using some modern equipment.

Time Required

45 minutes

Materials

- 3 bright flashlights
- 3 rubber bands
- square piece of red cellophane about 6 in. (15 cm) on a side
- square piece of green cellophane about 6 in. (15 cm) on a side
- square piece of blue cellophane about 6 in. (15 cm) on a side
- sheet of white copier paper
- compact disc (CD)
- masking tape
- table or counter next to a wall in a room that can be made dark

Safety Note No special safety precautions are needed for this activity. Please review and follow the safety guidelines before proceeding.

Procedure

1. Use the masking tape to secure the white piece of paper to the wall directly above the top of the table or counter. The paper will serve as a screen. Make the room as dark as possible. Turn on the flashlight and shine it at the paper. Observe the spot of light produced by the flashlight. Hold the flashlight in one hand and the CD in the other. Shine the flashlight so it reflects (bounces off) the back of the CD. Angle the CD so that the reflected light strikes the white piece of paper. (See Figure 1.) Observe the spot of light coming off the CD.

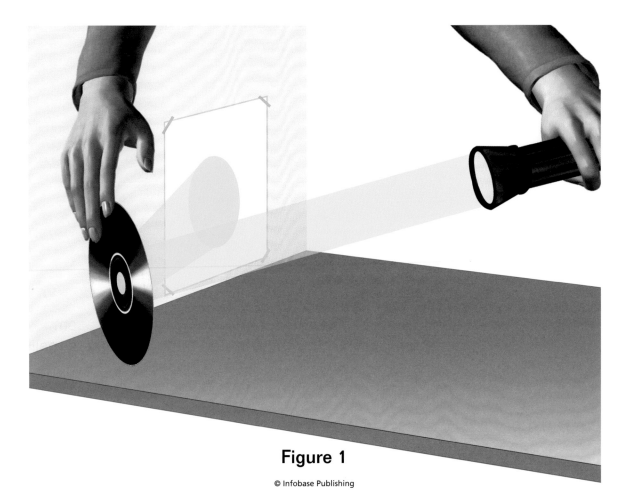

Figure 1

© Infobase Publishing

2. Use a rubber band to secure the red piece of cellophane over the lens of the flashlight. Cover the lens of the second flashlight with blue cellophane, and cover the third flashlight with green cellophane. Shine the red-covered flashlight at the white paper, and observe the spot. Then, shine

the red-covered flashlight at the CD as you did in Step 1, and observe the reflected beam as it strikes the white paper. Repeat the procedure with the blue- and green-covered flashlights, and observe the results.

3. Turn on the red-covered flashlight and place it flat on the table so that the beam strikes the white paper. Do the same with the blue-covered flashlight, angling it so that the two light spots overlap on the white paper. Observe the spot produced by the two beams. Repeat the procedure using the red- and green-covered flashlights and the green- and blue-covered flashlights.

4. Turn on all three flashlights and place them flat on the table facing the white paper. Angle them so that the ends of their beams overlap on the white paper. Observe the color of the spot.

Analysis

1. What color was the spot produced by the plain (uncovered) flashlight when it hit the white paper on the wall? What happened to the color of the flashlight beam after you bounced it off the CD?

2. How did the colors produced by the red-, blue-, and green-covered flashlights compare with the colors produced by their beams after they were bounced off the CD?

3. How did the spot of light look when you mixed the red- and blue-covered flashlight beams on the white paper? What about when you mixed the green- and blue-covered flashlight beams? What color was the spot when you mixed all three colored beams together?

 ## What's Going On?

When Isaac Newton did his famous experiment using a prism and a beam of sunlight, he demonstrated that white light is really a blend of seven colors: red, orange, yellow, green, blue, indigo, and violet. Today, most scientists agree that the visible light spectrum has only six true colors with indigo being omitted. Each color of light has a different wavelength and frequency. A prism separates the colors using a process called **refraction**. As the beam of white light passes through the prism, each color of light is refracted, or bent, a different amount. The red light bends the least and the violet light bends the most. A CD also splits light, but through a process called diffraction.

Placing the colored cellophane over the lens of a flashlight changes the color of the light. The cellophane acts like a filter, stopping all the frequencies of light but one. The flashlight covered with the red cellophane made a red spot because only red light could pass through the red cellophane. All the other colors were stopped. Light of one color is called monochromatic. When you shined the red light on the CD, it should have produced only reddish colors.

In the final step of the experiment, you showed that different colors of light could be blended to make new colors. Mixing red and blue light produced a purplish color called magenta. Mixing red and green light produced yellow. Mixing blue light and green light produces a bluish color called cyan. Mixing red, blue, and green light produced white light. It is important to note that mixing different colors of light is different from mixing different colors of paint. If you mix red, blue, and green paint together, you get dark brown or even black.

Our Findings

1. The flashlight alone produced a white spot. The beam reflected off the CD produced a rainbow.

2. The red-covered flashlight produced a red spot. The red beam from reflecting off the CD also produced a red color. The blue-covered flashlight produced a blue spot. The blue beam reflecting off the CD also produced a blue color. The green-covered flashlight produced a green spot. The green beam reflecting off the CD also produced a green color.

3. The red- and blue-covered flashlights together produced a purple spot. The red- and green-covered flashlights produced a yellow spot. The green- and blue-covered flashlights produced a cyan spot. All three flashlights shining together produced a white spot.

THE POWER OF PIGMENTS

In the previous experiment we saw how a beam of white light could be dispersed or separated into a spectrum of colors. You also demonstrated how a beam of white light could be filtered to produce a single color of light. Neither of these actions fully explains how a pigment works though. We previously mentioned that pigments are materials that give paint its color. Pigments aren't found just in paint and dyes. Natural pigments are found in anything that has color. An apple appears red and a blueberry appears blue because of the pigments in their skins. Pigments produce colors somewhat like filters do. Yet, instead of allowing only certain frequencies of light to pass through them, they allow only certain frequencies of light to bounce off their surface. In **Experiment 9:** *How Light Affects Pigments,* you will discover how the type of light, in addition to the color of a pigment, controls the color you see.

EXPERIMENT 9

How Light Affects Pigments

Topic

How do pigments interact with different colored light to produce a final color?

Introduction

When it comes to painting a picture, choosing the right colored paints is only part of the process. In order to get the picture just right, an artist will work hard to find just the "right" light. In this activity, you will test to see how changing the light under which a picture is viewed can have a major impact on the colors you see. Important note: For this experiment to be successful, you must have a totally dark room.

Time Required

45 minutes

Materials

- 2 bright flashlights
- 2 rubber bands
- square piece of dark red cellophane about 6 in. (15 cm) on a side
- square piece of dark green cellophane about 6 in. (15 cm) on a side
- 2 sheets of white copier paper
- red marker
- green marker
- box of crayons, colored pencils, or markers with at least seven different colors
- room that can be made totally dark (a closet will work, too)

Red cellophane
wrapped over lens

Rubber band

Figure 1

© Infobase Publishing

Procedure

1. Use a rubber band to secure the red cellophane over the lens of one flashlight. Cover the lens of the second flashlight with green cellophane.

2. Use the green marker to print your name across one sheet of white paper. Take the red marker and completely color over your name. Using the crayons, colored pencils, or markers, write the word *science* in bold letters across the second piece of paper. Use a different color for each letter. When you are finished, record the names of the colors you used for each letter.

3. Place the two pieces of paper with writing on them side by side. Make the room as dark as possible. Turn on the red-covered flashlight and shine it on the two pieces of paper. Record the colors that you see. Turn off the red-covered flashlight and turn on the green-covered one. Repeat the procedure. Turn on both flashlights and shine them simultaneously on each piece of paper. Record what you see.

Analysis

1. What happened to the colors of the word *science* when you viewed it under the red light? The green light?

2. What happened to the colors in the word *science* when you viewed them under both flashlights together?

3. What happened to your name when you viewed it under red light? When you viewed it under green light? When you viewed it under red and green light together?

What's Going On?

When white light is passed through a red filter, only those frequencies that produce red light will pass through. The rest are blocked or absorbed. Pigments do the same thing as filters. However, instead of allowing certain colors of light to pass through them, they allow only certain light frequencies to bounce off their surfaces. An apple appears red because pigments in its skin absorb all the frequencies of light except for those in the red part of the spectrum, which are reflected.

Most of the time, we view objects under white light. As a result, the colors we see are controlled by the pigments in their surfaces. When objects are viewed under light that is not white, both the pigments and the light control the colors we see. In this experiment, the red and green cellophane filtered the light coming out of the flashlights. When you viewed your name under the red light, you saw a red spot and the letters of your name in black underneath. This was because the red light coming from the flashlight reflected off the red pigment on top of the letters and was absorbed by the green pigment of the letters. Because there was no green light hitting the green letters, they could not reflect green. Instead, they looked black because they absorbed all of the red light. When you switched to green light, all you could see was a large dark spot with no letters underneath. This was because the green light was hitting the red pigment. Red pigment can reflect only red light. Because the red pigment absorbed the green light, the spot was black. No light reached the green letters underneath, so they were invisible.

Our Findings

1. When compared with the original colors, the colors of the letters in the word *science* should have appeared different under the red light than under the green light.
2. When viewed under the red and green lights together, the colors of the letters in the word *science* should have been closer to the original colors.

3. When viewed with the red flashlight, you should have seen the red spot over your name, and the letters should have appeared black. When viewed under green light, your name should have disappeared, and you should have seen a black spot. When you viewed your name with both flashlights, you should have seen green letters under a red spot.

CLOTHES OF A DIFFERENT COLOR

Have you ever tried on clothes at a store and then had them change color when you got home or stepped outside? The color change has nothing to do with the clothes. It's all because of the light under which you are viewing them. Though both the light from the Sun and a standard light bulb appear white, they do not have the exact same blend of colors. Some light sources are a little bluer, while others are a little redder. As a result, the pigments found in the dyes that color your clothes reflect slightly different colors.

If you have ever visited an art museum, you have probably noticed that many of the paintings are illuminated by special light sources. Quite often these lights contain "daylight" bulbs. These bulbs are specially made to have a blend of light frequencies that matches sunlight. When artists paint pictures, they usually do so in sunlight. In order to make the colors in the painting appear the way the artists originally intended, the light in the museum has to match the light in which they were painted.

When artists paint, the light they use isn't the only thing they worry about. They are also choosy about the paint colors. In many cases, they will mix their own colors, using a set of stock pigments. In **Experiment 10:** *Mixing Pigments*, you will discover how a simple set of pigments can produce a wide range of colors.

EXPERIMENT 10 Mixing Pigments

Topic

What happens when pigments are mixed together?

Introduction

Pigments are the materials found in paints and dyes which give them their color. Art supply stores have thousands of different paint colors. If you look closely, however, you'll find that there are very few pure colors. Most paints are slight variations on a primary color, so instead of just plain red, there are reds that contain some orange, pink, or purple. Artists often blend different paints to create new colors. In this activity, you will experiment with mixing pigments to determine how many colors you can make.

Time Required

60 minutes

Materials

● 3 medium-sized (8 oz) clear plastic cups

● 16 small (3 oz) paper bathroom cups

● 3 medicine droppers

● red, blue, and yellow food coloring

● water

● black marker

● paper towels for spills

● table or counter to work on

Safety Note No special safety precautions are needed for this activity. Please review and follow the safety guidelines before proceeding.

Procedure

1. Put five drops of red food coloring in the bottom of one of the clear plastic cups. Fill the cup with water. Repeat the procedure with the blue food coloring in the second cup and with the yellow food coloring in the last plastic cup. Place one medicine dropper in each cup.

| Cup 1 | Cup 2 | Cup 3 | Cup 4 |
| 2R,8B | 4R,6B | 6R,4B | 8R,2B |

| Cup 5 | Cup 6 | Cup 7 | Cup 8 |
| 2R,8Y | 4R,6Y | 6R,4Y | 8R,2Y |

| Cup 9 | Cup 10 | Cup 11 | Cup 12 |
| 2B,8Y | 4B,6Y | 6B,4Y | 8B,2Y |

| Cup 13 | Cup 14 | Cup 15 | Cup 16 |
| 2B,4R,4Y | 4B,2R,4Y | 4B,4R,2Y | 4B,4R,4Y |

Figure 1

2. Use the black marker to label the outside of the 16 paper cups as shown in Figure 1.

3. Lay out the labeled cups on the table using the grid shown in Figure 1. In this grid, *R* stands for red, *B* stands for blue, and *Y* stands for yellow. Using the medicine droppers, mix the colors according to the labeled codes. For example, in Cup 1, mix two drops of red water with eight drops of blue water. In Cup 2, mix four drops of red water with six drops of blue water. After you have completed all 16 mixtures, observe the colors in each of the paper cups.

Analysis

1. What color did you make when you mixed the red and blue water?

2. What color did you make when you mixed the red and yellow water?

3. What color did you make when you mixed yellow and blue water?

4. What happened to the different colors as you varied the amount of pigment in each?

5. What color did you make when you mixed all three colors of water in Cup 16?

 What's Going On?

Pigments work by absorbing or soaking up some of the frequencies found in visible light and reflecting others. A red car, for example, appears red because the pigment in the paint reflects only the frequencies that match red light. All of the other frequencies of light striking the car are absorbed by the paint.

Back in the 1600s, Sir Isaac Newton discovered that different colors of light could be blended together to make other colors. If you mix red, blue, and green light together, the result will be white light. That's because the frequencies of light are added together. This is known as an additive process. Pigments work in exactly the opposite way. Because each pigment absorbs some of the frequencies of light, mixing a large number of pigments yields black or a muddy brown color. Mixing pigments is a subtractive process because each pigment removes or subtracts some of the frequencies of light.

Artists and printers use the subtractive property of pigments to mix a wide range of colors of paints, inks, and dyes. The three primary pigment colors are cyan (a type of blue), magenta (a pinkish red), and yellow. By using these three colors in different proportions, it is possible to create millions of colors, including black. One of the few colors that cannot be created by mixing the three primary pigments is white.

Our Findings

1. The red and blue water made a purple color when they werer mixed.
2. The red and yellow water made an orange color when they were mixed.
3. The yellow and blue water made a green color when they were mixed.
4. Changing the relative mix of pigments gave a color a lighter or darker shade.
5. When all three colors of water were mixed, they made a dark brown color.

COLOR WHEELS AND COMPLEMENTARY COLORS

Though modern artists have thousands of manufactured paints to choose from, many still prefer to mix their own colors. As we saw in the previous experiment, even slight variations in pigments can produce a dramatic change in the color of paint. Before mixing paints, many artists will test out new blends on something called a color wheel. A color wheel looks like a circle that has been divided into six wedges.

The artist begins by filling in three of the wedges with some variation of one of the three primary colors, skipping a wedge between each. For example, the top wedge would be sky blue, the lower right wedge would be sunset red, and the lower left

Color Wheel

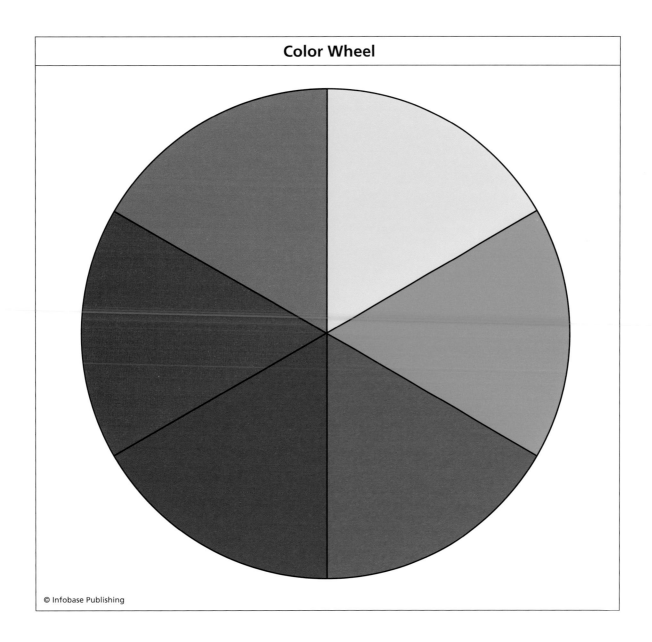

wedge would be banana yellow. There are empty spaces on both sides of each colored wedge. The artist will then mix two adjacent colors to fill the wedge between them. This produces three blended colors. It then gives an artist a chance to evaluate both primary and complementary colors. A complementary color is the one directly opposite a selected color on the color wheel. For example, in the aforementioned wheel, red's complementary color would be a shade of green, and blue's complementary color would be some type of orange. Artists will often mix a complementary color with a primary color to produce an even wider range of colors.

COLOR SEPARATION

Mixing pigments allows an artist to produce new colors. But once they are mixed together, can pigments ever be separated? As it turns out, the answer is yes. In **Experiment 11:** *Separating Pigments*, you will separate several different colors to determine which pigments were used to make the main color mix.

EXPERIMENT 11

Separating Pigments

Topic

How can pigments be separated?

Introduction

Pigments give paints and dyes their color. Artists often blend pigments to create new colors. Though two colors of paint may look similar to the eye, they can result from different blends of pigments. In this activity, you will use a process called chromatography to separate inks with similar colors. This will expose the colors used to produce each ink.

Time Required

45 minutes

Materials

- 6 large disposable plastic cups
- 6 pencils
- plain white paper towel
- cellophane tape
- scissors
- ruler
- water
- 3 thin black water-based felt-tipped markers, each a different brand (e.g., Flair, Pilot, Vis-a-Vis)
- 3 thin red water-based felt-tipped markers, each a different brand (e.g., Flair, Pilot, Vis-A-Vis)
- table or counter to work on

> **Safety Note** No special safety precautions are needed for this activity. Please review and follow the safety guidelines before proceeding.

Procedure

1. Use the scissors to cut six strips out of the paper towel, each 6 in. long by 1 in. wide (15 cm by 2.5 cm). With one red marker, draw a thin line across one of the paper strips 1 in. (2.5 cm) from the bottom. In pencil, write the brand of the marker across the top of the strip. Repeat the procedure with the other red markers and the three black markers. When you are finished, you should have six strips of paper towel, each with a line drawn with a different marker. Carefully observe the lines and look for any color differences.

2. Fill each large plastic cup with ½ in. (1 cm) of water. Take one strip of paper towel and lower it into the cup with the line end down. The bottom of the paper should just touch the water. The line should not touch the water. Put one of the pencils across the top of the cup. Tape the top of the paper strip to the pencil. It should look like Figure 1. Repeat this procedure with

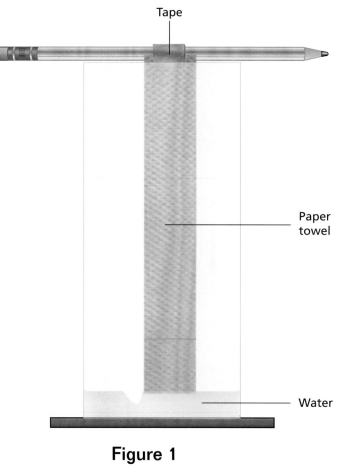

Tape

Paper towel

Water

Figure 1

the other five paper strips. Allow the cups to sit undisturbed for about 15 minutes.

3. Lift each paper towel strip out of the cup by the pencil. Look at the colors on the strips and note how they compare with the original ones.

Analysis

1. How did the colors on the three red-lined strips compare with one another before you placed them in the water?

2. What happened to the lines on the paper strips when they were placed in the cups with water?

3. What colors were present in the red-lined strips after they soaked in the water?

4. What colors were present in the black-lined strips after they soaked in the water?

 ## What's Going On?

When it comes to commercially produced inks, paints, and dyes, there are almost no pure colors. In this experiment, you used a process known as paper chromatography to separate the pigments found in the red and black ink of three different brands of marker. Chromatography works on the principle that each pigment has a slightly different density. Commercial ink is made by blending different pigments together. In general, each brand of marker has a unique formula of ink. Red is one of the primary colors of the visible light spectrum. As a result, the pigments found in red ink are mostly shades of red, but they may also include a small amount of orange and yellow. Black, on the other hand, is the result of many colors mixing together. When black ink is separated, you find a much wider range of colors. Two different brands of marker may produce black lines that look the same, but an analysis of the ink will usually reveal different mixes of pigments.

Our Findings

1. Before getting wet, all three red lines should have had a similar color.

2. Once the bottom of the paper strips got wet, the water moved up the strip separating the colors.

3. Answers will vary, but in addition to red, there may have also been orange and yellow.

4. You should have seen a wide range of colors, including red, yellow, blue, purple, orange, and brown.

COLOR PRINTING

Color blending and separation are important in the printing of color pictures and photographs. If you use a magnifying glass to examine a color photo in a magazine or newspaper, you'll see that it's actually made up of thousands of tiny dots. From a distance, the picture may appear to have dozens of colors in it, but the dots that make up the picture are only four colors: magenta, cyan, yellow, and black. Your eyes make the other colors by blending the different pigments together.

Before a color picture can be printed, the original image is split into the three primary colors. This is done by photographing the image three times through yellow, cyan, and magenta filters. Each of the three single-color negatives has a different distribution of color, based on the original colors in the image. The negatives are then used to transfer ink onto metal plates, which are then used to print the picture. Although printers have used this technique for many years, modern technology allows you to do something similar in your own home. Every time you print a color picture from your computer using an inkjet printer, you are using the same color blending process. Just look at the picture closely and you'll see a lot of dots!

Capturing Images

Whether it's a painter creating a portrait or a tourist snapping a photo of a famous landmark, capturing of an image is one of the most common themes in art. In order for us to see an image, light has to reach our eyes. Before that light can get to our eyes, however, it must first reflect off something. As it turns out, there's more than one way to reflect light. In ***Experiment 12: Diffuse vs. Regular Reflection***, you will experiment with several types of reflection and see how they control how an artist views and captures an image.

EXPERIMENT 12
Diffuse vs. Regular Reflection

Topic

What is the difference between diffuse and regular reflection and how do these types of reflection affect what we see?

Introduction

The word *reflection* has several meanings. Most often, when we speak about seeing our reflection, we're referring to our own likeness as seen in a mirror. The word also can describe the way light bounces off an object. If it were not for the reflection of light, we would not see anything. In this activity, you are going to compare two types of reflection to see how they affect the way an image appears.

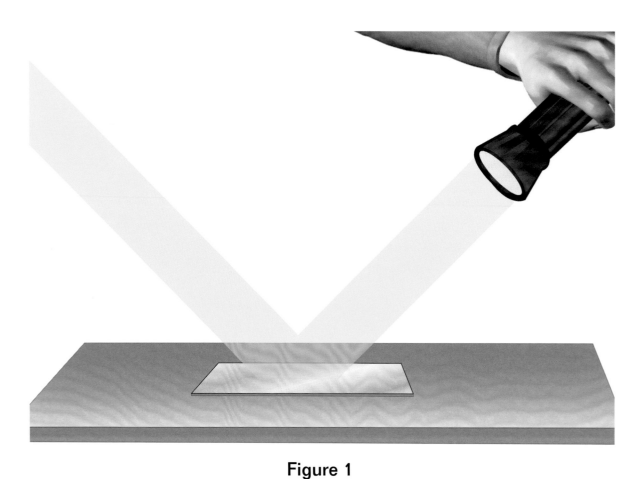

Figure 1

Time Required

30 minutes

Materials

- multiple bright flashlights
- flat mirror
- roll of aluminum foil
- table or counter
- room that can be made totally dark (a closet will work, too)

Safety Note No special safety precautions are needed for this activity. Please review and follow the safety guidelines before proceeding.

Procedure

1. Place the mirror flat on the table in front of you, reflective side up. Look in the mirror and observe your reflection. Make the room as dark a possible, and then look in the mirror again. Record your observations.

2. Turn on the flashlight and hold it above the mirror so that the beam is pointing straight down. Observe which way the beam bounces off the mirror. Slowly tilt the flashlight so that instead of pointing straight down, it is striking the mirror at about a 45-degree angle (see Figure 1). Observe the direction in which the beam bounces off the mirror. Tilt the flashlight in the opposite direction, and continue to observe the beam.

3. Turn the lights on, and tear off a piece of aluminum foil from the roll, making sure not to wrinkle it. Place the foil on the table in front of you, shiny side up. Look down into the foil and observe your reflection. Compare it with the way your reflection looked in the mirror in Step 1.

4. Make the room as dark as possible, and turn on the flashlight. Shine the flashlight into the foil as you did with the mirror in Step 2. Compare the way the beam of light hits and bounces off the foil with the way it behaved when it hit the mirror.

5. Turn the lights back on again, and grasp the piece of foil by the edges. Gently wrinkle the foil. Look down into the foil again and observe your reflection. Compare it with the way it looked in Step 3.

6. Make the room as dark as possible, and shine the flashlight into the wrinkled foil as you did in Step 4. Compare the way the beam of light bounces off the wrinkled foil with the way it did with the smooth foil.

Analysis

1. How did your reflection in the mirror change when you changed the room from light to dark?

2. How did the angle of the beam bouncing off the mirror compare with the angle of the beam striking the mirror?

3. How did your reflection in the smooth foil compare with your reflection in the mirror?

4. How did the beam of light bouncing off the smooth foil compare with the beam of light bouncing off the mirror?

5. How did your reflection in the wrinkled foil compare with your reflection in the smooth foil?

6. How did the beam of light bouncing off the wrinkled foil compare with the beam bouncing off the smooth foil and the mirror?

 What's Going On?

When light reflects or bounces off a surface, it does so in two very different ways. When you see your reflection in a mirror, it is due to a phenomenon called regular reflection. Regular reflection occurs with smooth, shiny surfaces such as a piece of glass, a shiny piece of smooth metal, a body of water without waves or ripples, and a flat mirror. When a beam of light hits a smooth, shiny surface, all of the light rays bounce off at the same angle. As a result, the beam of light stays intact. You can see this if you shine a flashlight into a flat mirror. No matter at what angle the light strikes the mirror, it bounces off at the exact same angle but in an opposite direction.

If a beam of light strikes a rough surface such as a brick wall or a person's face, it will still bounce off. However, instead of the reflected rays traveling in the same direction, they scatter in different directions. This is known as diffuse reflection. When you look at a brick wall, instead of seeing the reflection of your face, you see the surface of the wall.

In this activity, you tested this concept using the mirror and the foil. When the beam from the flashlight hit the mirror, you could clearly see the spot bouncing off it. When the beam from the flashlight hit the smooth foil, the spot bouncing off of it was still visible, although not as clearly defined. Though the foil was shiny, it was not as smooth as the mirror. Once the foil was wrinkled, the beam from the flashlight simply lit up the foil and scattered. No reflected spot was visible. In our daily lives, diffuse reflection is far more common than regular reflection. If it were not for diffuse reflection, objects would be invisible.

Our Findings

1. When the room was dark, the reflection in the mirror disappeared.
2. At whatever angle the light hit the mirror, the beam bounced off at the same angle in the opposite direction.
3. The reflection in the smooth foil was not as clear as it was in the mirror.
4. The spot of light bouncing off the smooth foil was not as distinct as the spot produced when the light bounced off the mirror.
5. After the foil was wrinkled, the image disappeared.
6. The spot of light bouncing off the wrinkled foil was scattered all over the room.

THE LAW OF REFLECTION

As we saw in the previous experiment, when a beam of light hits a mirror, it behaves in a predictable way. When the beam strikes the mirror at a certain angle, it will bounce off at the same angle, but in the opposite direction. Scientists call this the law of reflection, and it is usually stated as follows: For a flat or planar mirror, the angle of incidence is equal to the angle of reflection. The law of reflection explains why mirrors do some interesting things to writing and images. If you hold up a sign with letters on it in front of a mirror, the letters in the reflection will appear backward—and so will the features of your face or any other reflected image. They are reversed because the light bounces off the mirror in the opposite direction.

Over the years, many artists have used mirrors to help them create their works, but no artist was more famous than Leonardo da Vinci. Leonardo was fascinated by mirrors and experimented with them frequently. Many of his journals and notebooks were written in "mirror writing"—they could be read only if held up to a mirror. Leonardo also used mirrors to explore **symmetry** in nature. He explored symmetry extensively in his paintings and sculptures. Symmetry happens when two sides of an object or image can be divided equally down the middle. In **Experiment 13:** *Exploring Symmetry*, you will use a mirror and drawings to make some of your own symmetry discoveries.

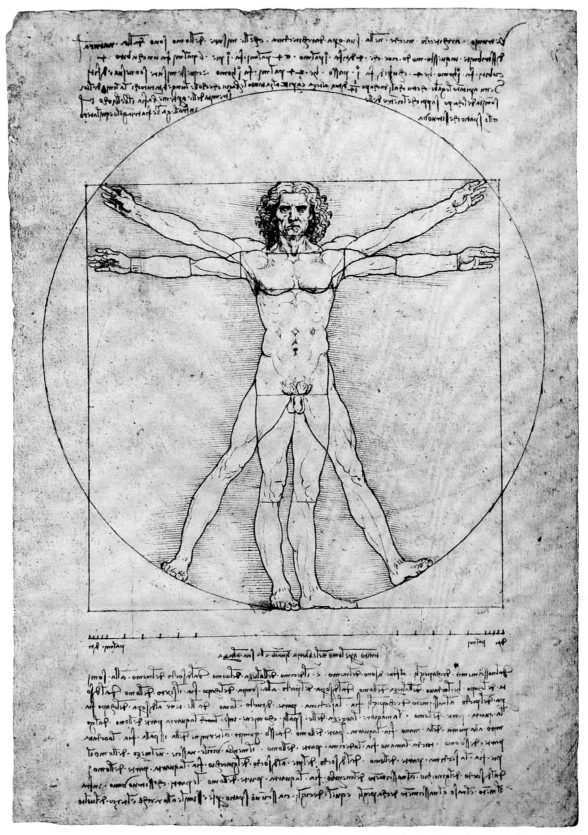

Leonardo da Vinci's interest in symmetry and proportion is exemplified in his Vitruvian man. The drawing represented the symmetry of the human body and, thus, the universe. It is meant to illustrate the connection between man and nature. The accompanying text was written in mirror-writing (backwards text that can easily be read in a mirror).

EXPERIMENT 13
Exploring Symmetry

Topic

What is symmetry, and how can it be created?

Introduction

Symmetry refers to an object or image having two equal parts. If you cut a circle in half, you will have two identical semicircles. The line that divides the circle is called the line of symmetry. In artwork, symmetry is used to balance a painting or sculpture. In architecture, symmetry is often used in structures. In this activity, you will use a mirror to create symmetrical images and to then find the line of symmetry in several common designs.

Time Required

45 minutes

Materials

- small, flat mirror
- large wall mirror
- ruler
- table or counter
- pencil
- white piece of copier paper

Safety Note No special safety precautions are needed for this activity. Please review and follow the safety guidelines before proceeding.

Procedure

1. Stand a few feet in front of the large wall mirror. Hold up your right hand with the palm facing the mirror. Lean forward so that your hand touches the mirror. Now step back from the mirror and extend both arms out in front of you. Turn the palms to face each other and slowly bring your hands together. Compare how your two hands look when they are touching each other to when you touched your right hand to the mirror.

2. Use the pencil and the ruler to draw a straight line down the middle of the paper. Place the paper on the table in front of you so that the line points at you. Take the small mirror and hold it up on edge. Place the mirror across the line so that the shiny side is facing you (see Figure 1). Slowly turn the mirror to the right and left, and look at the reflection of the line in the mirror. Compare the image of the line in the mirror to the line on the paper.

Figure 1

© Infobase Publishing

3. Look at Figure 2. Following the same procedure as in Step 2, hold the mirror horizontally across the middle of the square. The mirror will act as a line of symmetry. Observe the image in the mirror (see Figure 2). Do the same for the triangle. Now hold the mirror vertically across the middle of the square and look at it from the side. Do the same for the triangle. Compare the images of the square and the triangle when observed in the mirror both horizontally and vertically.

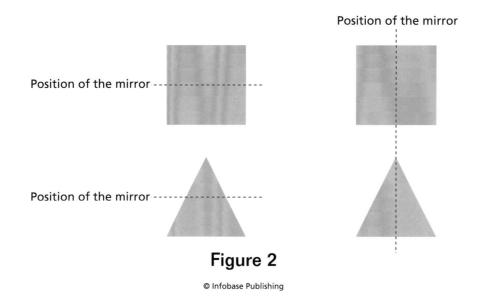

Figure 2

© Infobase Publishing

4. Using capital block letters write the word *apple* across the middle of the paper. Below it write the word *OHIO*. Place the mirror on edge and hold it horizontally above the word *APPLE* so that you can read the letters in the mirror. Compare the letters on the paper with the image of the letters in the mirror. Next, hold the mirror vertically so that it is next to the *E* in the word *apple* and look in the mirror from the side so that you can observe the letters. Compare the letters on the paper with the image of the letters in the mirror. Repeat the same procedure for the word *OHIO,* and compare your results.

Analysis

1. How did the image of the line in the mirror compare with the line drawn on the paper when you moved the mirror back and forth across it?
2. What was the result when you used the mirror to cut the square in half horizontally and vertically?
3. What was the result when you used the mirror to cut the triangle in half horizontally and vertically?
4. How did the letters in the word *APPLE* compare with the letters in the word *OHIO* when you observed them horizontally in a mirror?
5. How did the letters in the two words compare when you viewed them vertically in the mirror?

What's Going On?

Many of the things we encounter in our everyday lives display symmetry. A brick, a basketball, a dog, and even a person all have what is known as bilateral symmetry. This means that the object can be cut in half along a line of symmetry and the two sides will be equal. You proved this in Step 1 of the activity. When you brought the palms of your hands together, they lined up perfectly. The same thing happened when you brought your right hand up to the mirror. If you were to divide your body in half vertically right down the middle, you would find that the right and left side were almost perfectly equal. They would be "mirror images" of each other.

Many common shapes also display symmetry. A circle can be cut in half in any direction and the two sides will be even. With a square, you can draw a line of symmetry horizontally across the center, vertically across the center and even diagonally from corner to corner. Like a square, a triangle displays vertical line symmetry but not horizontal line symmetry. Dividing it horizontally, you produce a six-sided figure. Many letters also display either vertical or horizontal line symmetry. In the word *APPLE*, the *E* has horizontal line symmetry and the *A* has vertical line symmetry. Thus, by looking at the word vertically as well as horizontally in a mirror, you'll see that only two letters look correct. The rest of the letters are asymmetrical. In the word *OHIO*, all the letters have both vertical and horizontal line symmetry. When you look at *OHIO* in a mirror in either direction, all the letters appear normal. The only other capital letter in the English alphabet to display both vertical and horizontal line symmetry is the *X*.

Our Findings

1. The line in the mirror was an exact copy of the line on the paper.

2. When the mirror was used to bisect the square, the image in the mirror coupled with the image on the paper produced a square in both directions.

3. When the mirror was used to bisect the triangle, the image in the mirror coupled with the image on the paper produced a triangle in the vertical direction but a six-sided figure in the horizontal direction.

4. When viewed in a mirror held horizontally, all of the letters in the word *APPLE* appeared upside down except for the letter *E.* All of the letters in the word *OHIO* appeared normal in the mirror.

5. When viewed in a mirror held vertically, all of the letters in the word *APPLE* appeared reversed except for the *A.* All of the letters in the word *OHIO* appeared normal in the mirror.

SIZE AND SCALE

In the previous experiment, we saw how symmetry brings a natural balance to the world. When artists draw or paint a picture, they frequently use symmetry to help balance the elements included in the work. For example, if there is a large tree on one side of a painting, the artist may place a building of a similar size on the other side. Often, an artist wants a piece to look asymmetrical. Purposely moving objects off center or having a large, open space on one side of the picture is one way an artist can direct the attention of the viewer to a particular detail. Another way is to manipulate the size and scale of the objects in the image. Placing objects in their correct **proportions** can be tricky. The term *proportion* refers to the relative size and shape of objects. In **Experiment 14:** *Maintaining Proportions at a Distance,* you will discover how size and distance work together to keep objects in their proper proportions.

Maintaining Proportions at a Distance

Topic

How do the proportions of objects change as you change your viewing distance?

Introduction

When an artist paints a picture, or when an architect designs a structure, he or she must pay close attention to the proportions of the elements in the design. A drawing of a man would look strange if his head were the same size as the rest of his body. In a similar fashion, a church wouldn't look quite right if the steeple were shorter than the front door. Proportions refer to the relative size of an object's length and width. In this activity, you will discover how changing the distance at which an object is viewed affects its apparent size but not its proportions.

Time Required:

30 minutes

Materials:

- large, hard-covered book (textbook)
- ruler
- tape measure or meter stick
- masking tape
- table or counter
- calculator

Safety Note   No special safety precautions are needed for this activity. Please review and follow the safety guidelines before proceeding.

Procedure

1. Measure the height and width of the book and record your measurements on the data table. Do not measure how thick the book is. Stand the book up and open it slightly so that it will stay upright on its own. Place the book at the front edge of the table (the side closest to you). Measure 10 ft (3 m) back from the edge of the table and mark that point on the floor with masking tape.

2. Stand with your feet together, your toes on the masking tape. Hold the ruler in your right hand with the zero mark pointing up and your thumb on top of the ruler. Stretch your arm straight out as far as it will go. Using Figure 1 as a guide, line up the top of the ruler with the top of the book on the table. Slide the tip of your thumb up or down the ruler until it exactly marks the bottom of the book. Read the distance between the top of the ruler and the tip of your thumb and record it on the data table under the heading "Book height at 10 feet." Repeat the same procedure to measure the width of the book, and record it under the heading "Book width at 10 feet."

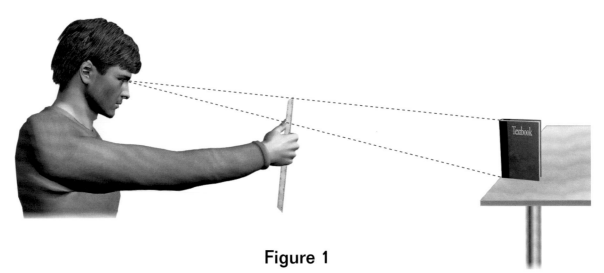

Figure 1

© Infobase Publishing

3. Measure 20 ft (6 m) from the edge of the table, and place a second piece of masking tape on the floor. Repeat Step 2, and record your measurements under the heading "Book height at 20 feet."

4. Using a calculator, divide the actual book height by the book width, and record the number on the data table. Do the same for the readings taken at 10 ft and 20 ft. Compare the results for each set of measurements.

Data Table 1		
Actual height of book	Height at 10 ft (3 m)	Height at 20 ft (6 m)
Actual width of book	Width at 10 ft (3 m)	Width at 20 ft (6 m)
Height/width	Height/width	Height/width

Analysis

1. Why must you hold your arm straight out when using the ruler to gauge the height and width of the book at a distance?
2. What happened to the apparent height and width of the book when you viewed it from 10 ft (3 m) away?
3. What happened to the apparent height and width of the book when you viewed it from 20 ft (6 m) away?
4. How did the height/width ratio compare in all three sets of measurements?
5. What happens to the apparent size of an object when it is viewed from a greater distance? What happens to the overall proportions of the object as the viewing distance changes?

 ## What's Going On?

In order to make pictures realistic, artists must always be concerned about the proportions of the objects they draw. For regular shaped objects, the proportions can be best described as the ratio of the object's height to its width. This figure is obtained by dividing the height by the width. As you observe an object from a greater distance, it appears to get smaller. The measurements of the height and width get smaller, but their ratio stays the same. By measuring objects and then calculating the height-to-width ratio, an artist can easily adjust the size of an object in a drawing to account for the distance at which it is viewed.

Our Findings

1. If you don't hold your arm in the exact same position for each measurement, the measured values will be incorrect.

2. When viewed from 10 ft (3 m), the height and width were smaller.

3. When viewed from 20 ft (6 m), the height and width were even smaller.

4. The ratio of height to width for all three sets of measurements should have been almost the same.

5. As the viewing distance increases, the apparent size of an object becomes smaller, but the proportions remain constant.

DEPTH AND THE THIRD DIMENSION

If you take a look around you, one of the first things you'll notice is that the images you see have depth. In other words, it's not a flat world. Some objects appear closer than others. We see depth because we view the world with two eyes that are spaced a few centimeters apart. When you view the world around you, each eye sends a separate signal—each with a slightly different field of view—to the brain. The brain takes these two images and merges them into one, three-dimensional image.

One of the biggest problems that early artists encountered was how to realistically depict depth and the third dimension in their pictures. Because paintings usually are done on a flat surface, normal depth perception would not be of any use. Early on, artists overlapped the objects in the picture. Things that were close were placed in the front of the picture, and more distant objects were behind them. To the viewer, this arrangement looked unnatural. What these images lacked was what we now call **perspective.**

Perspective is the method that artists use to give an image the appearance of depth. It is based on the Latin word *perspicere* which means "to see through." The use of perspective gives the viewers the sense that they are looking at a scene through a window. In **Experiment 15:** *How Image Depth Affects Perspective*, you will try your hand at using this scientific technique to add a little depth to a simple drawing.

EXPERIMENT 15

How Image Depth Affects Perspective

Topic

How can perspective give the appearance of depth to an image?

Introduction

Linear perspective is one method artists use to create the illusion of depth. The simplest form is known as one-point perspective. This method creates a vanishing point at which objects in the distance seem to disappear on the horizon. The horizon is defined as the line at which the sky and ground appear to meet. There is also a vantage point—the place from which the viewer is looking. In this activity, you will draw two identical pictures—one with perspective and one without—to discover how using some basic rules of geometry can add depth to an image.

Time Required

45 minutes

Materials

- 2 books, cereal boxes, blocks, or similar rectangular objects that are both the same size
- ruler
- meter stick or tape measure
- large rectangular table cleared of any objects
- pencil
- 2 pieces of plain white copier paper

Safety Note No special safety precautions are needed for this activity. Please review and follow the safety guidelines before proceeding.

Procedure

1. Stand at one of the shorter sides of the table. The long axis of the table should point directly away from you. Place one object at the right side of the table directly on the front edge. This will be object A. Place the second object at the left side of the table on the rear edge. This will be object B. The setup should look like Figure 1.

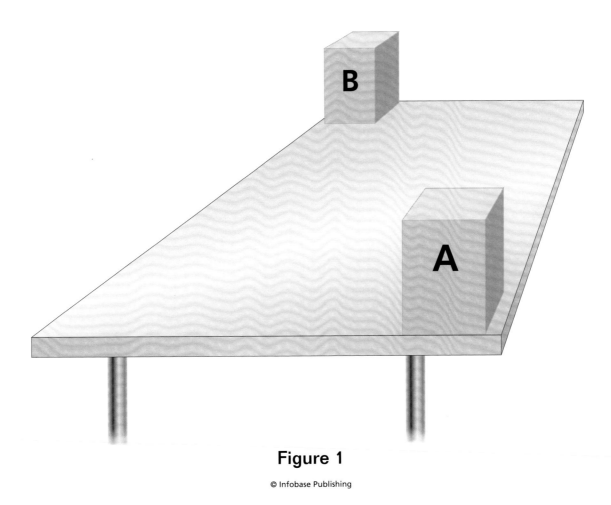

Figure 1

2. Measure the height and width of the two objects on the table. Also measure the length, width, and height of the table. Record this information on the data table under the heading "True Dimensions."

3. Stand 10 ft (3 m) from the front edge of the table. Hold the ruler in your right hand with the zero mark pointing up and your thumb on top of the ruler. Stretch your arm straight out as far as it will go. Using Figure 2 as a guide, line up the top of the ruler with the top of object A. Slide the tip of your thumb up or down the ruler until it exactly marks the bottom of the object. Read the distance between the top of the ruler and the tip of

your thumb and record it on the data table under the heading "Apparent dimensions viewed at 10 feet." Repeat the same procedure to measure the width of object A, the height and width of object B, and the height and width of the table. When making your measurements, measure both the front edge and the rear edge of the table, as well as the apparent height of the front leg and the rear leg.

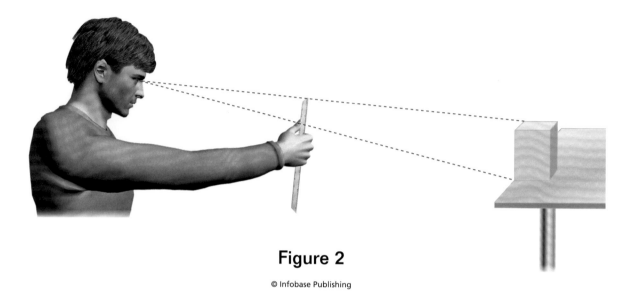

Figure 2

© Infobase Publishing

4. Place the first piece of paper on the table with the short edge closest to you. Measure 3 in. (8 cm) from the top of the page and draw a horizontal line across the page. This line will be the horizon line. Measure 3 in. (8

Figure 3

© Infobase Publishing

cm) from the left edge of the paper and draw a vertical line from the bottom of the page to the horizon line. Measure 3 in. (8 cm) from the right edge of the paper and draw a vertical line from the bottom of the page to the horizon line. The two lines will represent a road. Draw a stick figure of a person at the bottom of the page on the right side of the road and a second person on the horizon line on the left side of the road. Make both figures the exact same height. The drawing should look like Figure 3.

5. Repeat Step 4 on the second piece of paper with the following changes: Before drawing the lines of the road, put a dot in the center of the horizon line (halfway between the right and left edges). Measure 3 in. (8 cm) from the left edge of the paper. At the bottom of the page, draw a line from this point to the dot on the center of the horizon line. Measure 3 in. (8 cm) from the right edge of the paper. At the bottom of the page, draw a line from this point to the same dot. Draw a stick figure of a person at the bottom of the page on the right side of the road and a second person on the horizon line on the left side of the road. Make the figure at the bottom of the page twice as tall as the figure on the horizon line. Compare this drawing with the first one you made.

Data Table 1	
True Dimensions	**Apparent Dimensions Viewed at 10 Feet**
Height of object A	Height of object A
Width of object A	Width of object A
Height of object B	Height of object B
Width of object B	Width of object B
Height of table	Height of table (front leg)

Width of table	Width of table (front edge)
	Height of table (rear leg)
	Width of table (rear edge)

Analysis

1. How did the true dimensions of object A compare with those of object B?

2. How did the apparent dimensions of object A compare with those of object B when they were viewed at a distance?

3. When viewed at a distance, how did the length of the front edge of the table compare with the length of the back edge of the table?

4. When viewed at a distance, how did the height of the front legs of the table compare with the height of the back legs of the table?

5. Which of your two drawings produced the better illusion of distance?

 ## What's Going On?

In order to make pictures realistic, artists often use perspective to produce the illusion of depth and distance. There are two rules when it comes to drawing with perspective. The first rule states that the farther away an object is from the viewer (vantage point), the smaller it will appear. You proved this by measuring the objects on the table. Although they had the same actual dimensions, the object at the back of the table appeared to be smaller than the object at the front.

The second rule says that depth is shown by lines that converge, or come together, in the distance. You proved this when you measured the front and rear edges of the table at a distance. Although these two edges were the same size, the rear edge appeared shorter than the front edge. If you were to draw the top of the table using the apparent dimensions, you would see that the two sides of the table would not be parallel (as they really are) but would appear to converge.

You put the two rules of perspective into practice when you made your second drawing of the road. In the first drawing, the two lines that represented the road were parallel, and the two figures were drawn to be the same size. In the second drawing, the two sides of the road were made to converge at a vanishing point on the horizon, and the figure that was farther away was drawn to be smaller. When you made your second drawing, you used perspective, which is why it gave a better sense of depth.

Our Findings

1. Object A and object B should have had the same dimensions.
2. Object A should have appeared larger than object B.
3. When viewed at a distance, the front edge of the table appeared longer than the rear edge of the table.
4. When viewed at a distance, the front legs of the table appeared longer than the rear legs of the table.
5. The drawing with the lines meeting at the horizon produced the better illusion of distance than the drawing with the parallel lines.

THE WORK OF M.C. ESCHER

Many artists have experimented with perspective, but M.C. Escher pushed it to the limit. Maurits Cornelis Escher was born in the Netherlands on June 17, 1898. The youngest son of a civil engineer, Escher enrolled in the School of Architecture and Decorative Arts in the Dutch city of Haarlem with

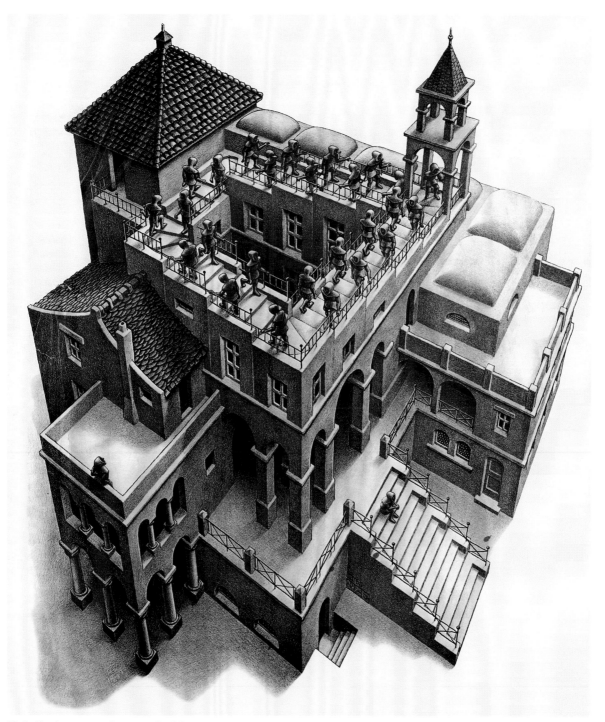

M.C. Escher experimented with symmetry and perspective in his art, including his famous Ascending and Descending, which features a never-ending staircase atop a building.

thoughts of following in his father's footsteps. He quickly found that his true love was not designing buildings but in drawing and graphic arts. After graduation, Escher moved to Italy, where he honed his drawing talents by completing hundreds of sketches of buildings and the Italian countryside. He became fascinated with the use of mathematics in art, including symmetry and perspective. It was at this point that he created his most famous works, drawing buildings with impossible angles and dimensions and symmetrical images depicting one type of animal morphing into another. Escher died in 1972, but he left a legacy that forever changed the way artists looked at and captured the world.

REFRACTION: THE BENDING OF LIGHT

As previously noted, passing a beam of white light through a prism splits the light into a spectrum of colors by a process called refraction. Refraction is the bending of a ray of light. It takes place any time light passes from one type of transparent material into another at an angle. In **Experiment 16:** *Refracting and Focusing Light*, you will discover how refraction happens and see how it can be put to use in the design of a lens.

EXPERIMENT 16 Refracting and Focusing Light

Topic

How can light be refracted and focused?

Introduction

When a beam of light travels from one transparent medium to another at an angle, it tends to bend, or refract. The refraction of light is responsible for many visual effects. When a beam of white light passes through a triangular prism, refraction causes the beam to spilt into its component colors. This splitting produces a spectrum. When you look at something with a magnifier, it appears larger because the magnifier refracts the light before it reaches your eye. In fact, if it were not for refraction, you would not be able to see. The lens of your eye refracts the light that enters it and brings it into focus on the retina. Microscopes, telescopes, binoculars, and cameras work due to the refraction of light. In this activity, you will test to see what factors affect refraction, and you will use a simple lens to bring a beam of light into focus.

Time Required

45 minutes

Materials

- 2 clear drinking glasses, each with a different diameter
- drinking straw
- water
- bright flashlight
- room that can be made dark (a closet will work, too)
- table or counter
- ruler

● pencil

● 3 plain white pieces of copier paper

Procedure

1. Fill the wider of the two drinking glasses half full with water. Hold the straw in the glass so that it is vertical. Observe the straw through the side of the glass. Slowly tilt the straw so that it is at an angle. Observe what happens to the straw as you tilt it. Hold the straw vertically again. Slowly move it forward so that it is touching the front of the glass. Move it backward until it touches the back of the glass. Do this several times and observe the straw as it moves. After you are finished, remove the straw from the glass and fill the second glass half full with water.

2. Lay one piece of paper flat on the table in front of you so that the long axis runs from right to left. Lay the flashlight so that its lens just touches the right side of the paper. The setup should look like Figure 1. Label the top of the paper "Light Without a Lens." Make the room as dark as possible and turn on the flashlight. Observe the beam of light as it travels across the paper. Use the pencil to trace the shape of the beam. Turn the room lights on and the flashlight off. Remove the paper.

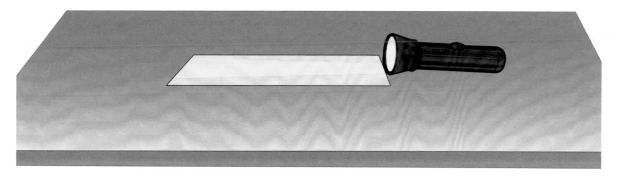

Figure 1

© Infobase Publishing

3. Put a second piece of paper in the same position next to the flashlight. Place the narrow glass of water directly in front of the flashlight lens. Label the top of the paper "Light Through a Narrow Lens." Make the room dark and turn on the flashlight. Observe the beam of light as it passes through the glass and over the paper. Use the pencil to trace the shape of the beam. Turn the room lights on and turn the flashlight off. Remove the paper.

4. Put the third piece of paper in the same position next to the flashlight. Take the wide glass of water and place it directly in front of the flashlight lens. Label the top of the paper "Light Through a Wide Lens," and repeat the procedure you followed in Step 3. When you are finished, turn the lights on again and compare the drawings.

Analysis

1. What happened to the straw as you tilted it from an upright position in the glass? How did the straw appear to change as you moved it from the front of the glass to the back?

2. What was the shape of the beam coming out of the flashlight without a lens?

3. What was the shape of the flashlight beam as it passed through the narrow glass?

4. What was the shape of the flashlight beam as it passed through the wide glass?

 ## What's Going On?

When a beam of light travels from one transparent substance to another, its speed changes. In the air, light travels at a speed of about 300,000 km/second (186,000 miles/s). In water, the speed slows to about 230,000 km/s (142,600 mi/s) If the beam of light enters the new material straight on, all of the light rays hit at the same time and change speed together. As a result, you don't see any change in the beam. If the beam enters the new material at an angle, however, some of the light rays hit before others do. They slow down first and are followed by the other rays. This makes the light beam bend.

When the straw in the glass was held vertically, it looked normal because all of the light rays were reaching your eye at the same time. When the straw was tilted, however, it appeared to "break" at the water line. The light coming from the straw under the water took a little longer to reach your eye than the light coming from the straw in the air.

When a transparent piece of glass or plastic has an angled or curved edge, it acts as a lens. Depending on the shape of a lens, it can either increase or decrease the apparent size of an object viewed through it. A circular glass of water is known as a biconvex lens. This is the same type of lens as a magnifier. When you looked at the straw vertically, it looked smaller as you moved it forward and larger as you moved it backwards in the glass. The greater the thickness of the lens (the more water you looked through) the larger the amount of magnification.

As the beam of light passes through the glass of water, the rays on the edge of the beam pass through less water. They are bent the most. The rays passing through the center of the glass are bent the least. Eventually, all of the rays meet at a single point. This is known as the focal point. The thicker the lens, the farther behind the lens is the focal point. The focal point is where the image is the brightest and clearest.

Our Findings

1. As the straw tilted, it appeared to "break" inside the glass where the water and air met. When the upright straw was held against the front of the glass, it looked normal. When the upright straw was moved to the back of the glass, the part in the water appeared to increase in size.

2. The beam coming out of the flashlight alone spread out in a cone across the paper.

3. After the beam of light passed through the narrow glass, some of the light rays were bent inward and then met at a point on the paper behind the glass.

4. After the beam of light passed through the wide glass, it had the same general shape as the light beam through the narrow glass, except the point at which the light rays converged was farther behind the glass.

CAMERAS BEFORE PHOTOGRAPHY

Over the centuries, painters have shown the uncanny ability to create pictures that are extremely lifelike. Yet, even the most talented artist cannot capture every detail. When an artist captures an image, there is always room for interpretation and error. The only way to capture a true reproduction of a scene or object is to take a photograph.

Many scientists, inventors, and artists attempted to create a device that could make an exact copy of an object or a scene, but it wasn't until the early 1800s that the process of photography became established. Along the way, a number of interesting developments occurred, including the invention of the camera obscura, a device that led to the modern camera. In **Experiment 17: *How a Camera Obscura Works,*** you are going to build a device that uses the same principles as a camera obscura to capture and focus an image.

EXPERIMENT 17
How a Camera Obscura Works

Topic

How does a camera obscura capture an image?

Introduction

Before cameras, artists used the camera obscura to help reproduce images of the world around them. The term *camera obscura* comes from a Latin phrase meaning "dark room." When the camera obscura was developed more than 1,000 years ago, it was nothing more than a darkened room with a small hole in one wall. As light entered through the hole, an image of the outside world was visible on the opposite wall. Later, people found that they could make portable versions, called pinhole cameras. In this activity, you will build a simple pinhole camera and discover how it works.

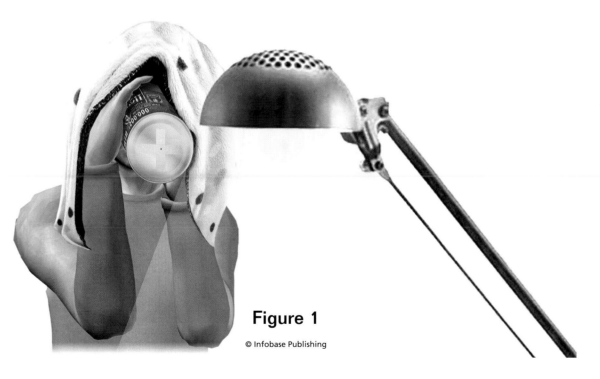

Figure 1

© Infobase Publishing

Time Required

45 minutes

Materials

- ☒ lamp with clear incandescent bulb

- ⬤ empty coffee can

- ⬤ thumbtack or pushpin

- ⬤ large nail that will create a $1/8$ in. (3 mm) hole

- ⬤ hammer

- ⬤ ruler

- ⬤ masking or some other type of opaque tape (not clear cellophane tape)

- ⬤ large rubber band

- ⬤ 12 in. x 12 in. (30 cm x 30 cm) sheet of wax paper

- ⬤ room or closet that can be made totally dark

- ⬤ person to assist you

- ⬤ blanket or large towel that light cannot pass through

> **Safety Note** Use caution when hammering the nail through the bottom of the coffee can. Do not look directly at the Sun with the pinhole camera. It is recommended that you conduct this activity under the supervision of a responsible adult.

Procedure

1. Place the coffee can on a sturdy table with the open end down. Use the hammer and nail to punch a hole in the bottom of the can at the center. The hole should be about $1/8$ in. (3 mm) in diameter. Remove the nail and cover the hole with a small piece of masking tape. Pierce a smaller hole in the tape with a thumbtack or pushpin, directly above the center of the nail hole.

2. Turn the can over and cover the opening with the wax paper. Stretch the paper tightly over the opening. Have your assistant secure the paper with the rubber band.

3. Darken the room and turn on the desk lamp. Stand about 3 ft (1 m) from the lamp, and point the bottom of the can toward the bulb in the lamp.

The light from the bulb will shine through the pinhole in the tape. You should see an image of the bulb on the wax paper. If you cannot get the room totally dark, cover your head and the paper-covered end of the coffee can with a blanket or towel to block out the light. (See Figure 1.)

4. While looking at the bulb, slowly move forward and backward. Observe what happens to the image of the bulb.

5. Remove the tape from the bottom of the can and repeat Steps 3 and 4, using the larger nail hole. Compare your observations with those you made through the pinhole.

Analysis

1. How did the image of the bulb appear on the wax paper screen when you first looked at it through the pinhole?

2. What effect did moving the can back and forth have on the image of the bulb on the wax paper screen?

3. How did the image of the bulb on the screen change when you looked at it through the larger nail hole?

 ## What's Going On?

Light rays coming from a point source—such as a candle, the Sun, or, in this case, a light bulb—travel in all directions in straight lines. As the light rays hit the bottom of the coffee can, most were blocked. Only a few went through the pinhole. As the rays passed through the hole, they crossed in space. This is why the image of the bulb was reversed.

When the tape was removed and you observed the bulb through a larger hole, the image of the bulb became brighter but less distinct. The larger hole allowed more light rays to enter the can and strike the paper. The image became fuzzier because the additional light rays interfered with one another as they passed through the opening.

Our Findings

1. The image of the bulb was dim and it appeared upside down.

2. Changing the viewing distance changed the size of the image. As you moved closer, the image of the bulb got larger.

3. Observing the bulb through the larger hole produced a brighter image, but the image was not as sharp.

MODERN DAY PHOTOGRAPHY

The scientific principles behind the camera obscura were discovered more than 1,000 years ago, but modern photography didn't come about until the early 1800s. People knew how to capture the image, but not how to record it. Film had not been invented, so the best that artists could do was to use the camera obscura to project an image on a screen and trace it. As you can imagine, this was time consuming and left room for errors. In the late 1700s, new discoveries in chemistry led to the development of the first photographic film.

Working in France, artist Joseph Niépce discovered that if he coated a metal plate with a substance called bitumen and then exposed the plate to the Sun, a negative image could be produced. In 1826, he used this process to take the first crude photograph of an outdoor scene. A few years later, Niépce teamed up with French businessman Louis Daguerre to create "daguerrotypes," which were permanent photographic images on metal plates. The real breakthrough came in 1840 when English scientist Henry Fox Talbot figured out a way to create a photographic negative. This negative could then be used to print multiple positive photographs on paper.

By the early 1870s, advances in cameras and lenses were making images much sharper, and the new art form of photography was sweeping the world. However, there was still one big problem: The processing of the photographs involved the use of toxic and explosive chemicals. In 1874, American scientist George Eastman, who founded Kodak, discovered how to secure the light-sensitive chemicals onto long strips of paper. The first true photographic film was born; with it, photography moved into the modern age.

These days, most cameras do not use film. Digital cameras were an outgrowth of the computer revolution. Instead of recording images on film, they record the images onto a computer chip. Digital cameras have spread so quickly that in June 2009, Kodak announced it would stop making their famous Kodachrome film due to the lack of demand.

The Art of Architecture

Up to this point, we've focused mainly on the science behind art forms. As it turns out, many of the scientific principles that apply to art also are found in architecture. The visual aspects of art—shadows, the reflection of light, symmetry, and perspective—are all important in architecture. In addition, architects use many of the same materials that artists do, including wood, stone, and clay. More than likely, it was through artistic activities, such as carving figures out of wood and stone and making pottery, that people discovered the properties of the building materials from which they would make their first structures.

Art and architecture are also closely related because they are both concerned with **aesthetics**, which is the way things appear. Anyone who has ever looked at a great cathedral, a towering skyscraper, or a delicately balanced suspension bridge knows that structures can also be works of art. The biggest difference between art and architecture concerns function. In addition to looking good, a building also has to serve a purpose and be structurally sound. After all, the most attractive building in the world cannot serve its purpose if it comes crashing down. A good architect must always balance form and function. To do so, he or she must have a good understanding of the forces of nature.

MAY THE FORCE BE WITH YOU

In simplest terms, a force can be thought of as something that exerts a pull or a push on an object. When it comes to designing a structure, architects deal with many forces, but **gravity** is the most important. From the tallest skyscraper to a simple mud hut, every building must withstand the force of gravity pulling it down to the surface of Earth. Other forces are created by the weather. Wind, rain, ice, and snow can all have serious impacts on a structure. Finally, there are also invisible forces, such as the chemical changes that occur in materials over time. Many bridges and barn roofs have come crashing down because of corroded metal or rotting wood.

Over the years, people have learned and adopted building techniques that help to overcome some of these destructive forces. In **Experiment 18:** *Building a Stable Brick Wall*, you will do a simple test to determine how to build a brick wall to best withstand the force of gravity.

EXPERIMENT 18
Building a Stable Brick Wall

Topic

What is the best way to build a structurally stable brick wall?

Introduction

If you have ever looked closely at a brick wall on the side of a building, you've probably noticed that the masons laid the bricks in a special pattern. Rather than stack the bricks directly on top of each other, they offset each new layer of bricks by half a brick. This makes the wall more visually appealing. But does it offer any structural advantages? In this activity, you will test two different methods of stacking bricks to see which helps to make a more stable wall.

Time Required

45 minutes

Materials

- 30 Lego® building blocks or interlocking building blocks of a similar style

- handheld blow dryer

- ruler

- table

Safety Note No special safety precautions are needed for this activity. Please review and follow the safety guidelines before proceeding.

Procedure

1. Use the building blocks to make three stacks, each 10 blocks high. When making the stacks, place each block directly on top of the one below it. Use the ruler to measure 12 in. (30 cm) from the edge of the table. Line up the three stacks of blocks next to one another at the far end of the ruler. They should form a wall parallel to the edge of the table. The setup should look like Figure 1.

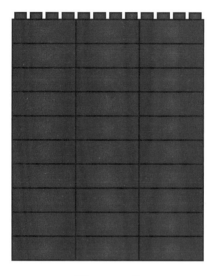

Figure 1

2. Place the zero end of the ruler in front of the blocks. The other end of the ruler should be even with the edge of the table. With the hair dryer on its highest speed setting, place the nozzle at the edge of the table, on top of the ruler. The nozzle should be directly in front of the block wall. Slowly slide the hair dryer closer to the block wall and watch the blocks. If any blocks fall over, stop moving the hair dryer and mark the spot on the ruler. Record this number, and then reset the blocks and the hairdryer to the original starting point. Repeat the procedure two more times to make certain that you get consistent numbers.

3. Take apart the three stacks of blocks and rebuild your wall so that it matches the wall shown in Figure 2. After you have completed the wall, repeat Step 2 using the new wall, and compare your results with those you recorded in the first set of trials.

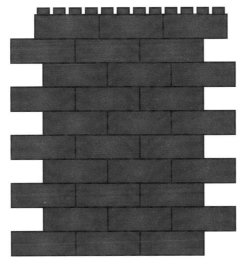

Figure 2

© Infobase Publishing

Analysis

1. Which stack of blocks fell farther away form the hair dryer?
2. How did the single-stacked bricks behave before they fell?
3. Which way of stacking blocks provides the most stability?

What's Going On?

As soon as children begin playing with building blocks, they quickly learn that there is a right way and a wrong way to stack them as far as stability is concerned. If equal-sized blocks are stacked directly on top of each other, the structure quickly becomes unstable. A small disturbance can topple them. When blocks are stacked so that each layer is offset from the one below it, the structure is much more stable. There are several reasons for the instability. First, as a wall gets taller, its center of mass gets higher. The center of mass of an object is the point at which all the mass appears to be concentrated. It is the location at which an object theoretically can be balanced. The higher an object's center of mass, the more unstable it becomes.

When you stack the blocks so that they are directly on top of each other, the center of mass rises directly over a single point of support. When you stack bricks in an offset manner, you are supporting the mass of a brick between two bricks below it, not just one. This helps to spread out the weight, which also lowers the center of mass. As a result, the wall becomes more stable. In the case of Legos, in which the bricks are interlocked, or bricks cemented together, the offset stacking also creates one single unit instead of many separate stacks, spreading out the base of support over a larger area.

Our Findings

1. The blocks that are stacked directly on top of each other usually fall much earlier.

2. Before they fell over, each section of the wall began to waver, independently of the others.

3. Stacking the blocks in an offset pattern makes the wall more stable because the entire wall acts as one large structural unit instead of several independent ones.

PYRAMIDS: ARCHITECTURAL WONDERS OF THE ANCIENT WORLD

Based on current archaeological evidence, the earliest large-scale, human-made structures discovered to date can be found in what is now Iraq. In the city of Tell Abu Shahrain (named Eridu when it was founded as the first city in southern Mesopotamia, circa 5400 B.C.) there are the remains of a great mud brick building called a *ziggurat*, which dates back to around 5000 B.C. A ziggurat is similar to a pyramid in design. It's wide at the base and gets narrow at the top. Yet, instead of smooth sloping sides like a typical Egyptian pyramid, a ziggurat rises in a series of steps.

A quick look at other ancient cultures reveals that many different people of the past also built pyramids. They can be found in India, Mexico, Greece, Central America, Sudan, and Ethiopia. Perhaps the most famous pyramid builders were the ancient Egyptians. Why did ancient architects design so many pyramids? Was it for purely aesthetic reasons, or did pyramids serve a practical function? In **Experiment 19:** *Building Pyramids*, you will test to see if a pyramid offers any advantages over other designs when it comes to building tall structures.

The Kukulcán Pyramid in Mexico is an example of a ziggurat. Though similar to a typical pyramid, each of a ziggurat's sides rise up in a succession of steps rather than in a flat slope.

EXPERIMENT 19

Building Pyramids

Topic

Does the design of a pyramid offer any structural advantages over other building types?

Introduction

One of the most common architectural designs in the ancient world is the pyramid. From Egypt to Central America, almost every ancient culture that built large permanent structures built them in a pyramid shape. In most cases, these pyramids were considered to be sacred places, serving primarily as temples and/or tombs. In this activity, you will build two structures and compare them to see if the design of a pyramid offers any structural advantages.

Time Required

60 minutes

Materials

- 150 Lego® blocks or similar interlocking building blocks all the same size
- table
- blow dryer
- bucket of fine dry sand (beach sand)
- dust mask

Safety Note   Step 1 of the procedure should be conducted outdoors so that it does not create any dust indoors. You should wear a dust mask when pouring the sand. Please review and follow the safety guidelines before proceeding.

Procedure

1. Find a location on the ground where it would be safe to dump the san-Pick up the bucket and slowly pour the sand onto the ground in one spot. Observe the shape that the sand makes as the pile gets bigger.

2. On the middle of the table build a tower seven blocks tall. Use the pattern in Figure 1. Turn the hair dryer on high and hold the nozzle 2 in. (5 cm) from the tower. Observe what happens to the tower. If the tower does not fall, add another level of blocks and repeat the procedure with the blow dryer. Continue adding blocks to the tower until you can knock it over with the hair dryer. Note how many blocks tall the tower is when it finally falls.

Figure 1

3. Take the tower apart and use the blocks to construct a pyramid. Lay out a square that has six blocks per side. (Note: For this to work, two opposite sides will have six full blocks and the other two opposite sides will have five whole blocks set between the first two sides). Add a second layer of blocks so that each new block is one half-block in toward the center of the square. Figure 2 shows this pattern. Continue to add layers of blocks until the pyramid is complete. The top level of the pyramid should contain only one block, and the entire pyramid should be 12 blocks high. Turn the hair dryer on high and point the nozzle directly at the top of the pyramid from a distance of 2 in. (5 cm). Compare what happens to the pyramid with what happened to the tower.

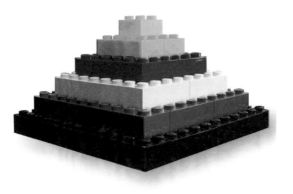

Figure 2

Analysis

1. What was the shape of the sand pile? What happened to the base of the pile as it got taller?
2. What happened to the tower right before it fell over?
3. What happened to the pyramid when you used the hair dryer on it?
4. Assuming that you were building a structure from heavy stone blocks, what other advantage would a pyramid have over a tower.

 ## What's Going On?

In Egypt, Mexico, and even on the streets of San Francisco (in the form of the skyscraper called the Transamerica Pyramid), pyramids are impressive structures. A pyramid is not only incredibly stable but also easy to build. The design of a pyramid mimics nature: Pyramids have a shape similar to most volcanoes and sand piles. All earth materials have a natural angle of repose at which they can remain stable on a slope against the pull of gravity. Once this angle is exceeded, the material begins to slide downhill. When you made the sand pile in Step 1, you should have noticed that as it became taller, it also became wider at the base. The angle of the slope remained fairly constant. The first pyramids were basically piles of brick or stone, so their designers took advantage of the angle of repose to keep them upright.

A pyramid also is stable because its wide base gives it a low center of gravity. The center of gravity of a structure is the point at which all the mass appears to be concentrated. You can think of the center of gravity as the tipping point. As long as there is adequate support under the center of gravity, the structure can remain standing. As a structure gets taller, its center of gravity gets higher. For a structure such as a tower, raising the center of gravity too much makes it top heavy and unstable. The smallest disturbance can make it come crashing down. Because of the way a pyramid is designed, if you make it taller, you also have to widen its base. As a result, the center of gravity never gets too high, and the structure remains stable.

There is one other practical reason why architects of the ancient world used the pyramid design for their tallest structures. The sides of a pyramid resemble an inclined plane or ramp. In order to get the building stones to the top levels of a pyramid, workers could simply drag them up a ramp supported by the lower levels of the pyramid itself. If they were to build a vertical tower, they would have had a difficult time lifting the stones to the top.

Our Findings

1. The sand made the shape of an inverted cone or a round pyramid. As the sand pile got higher, its base became wider.
2. Before it fell over, the tower became unsteady and began to wobble back and forth.
3. The pyramid was not affected at all by air coming from the hair dryer.
4. The pyramid's steplike sides would make it much easier to move heavy stones up to the top. The shape of the pyramid is the same as that of an inclined plane or ramp. A tower would require that the stones be lifted straight up.

IMHOTEP: ARCHITECT OF THE PYRAMIDS

As you might have guessed, the pyramids of Egypt weren't built by a group of people randomly stacking stones together. It took a great deal of planning and precision engineering to create these architectural marvels. Unfortunately, the records from the times when the pyramids were built are quite spotty, and there is still a great debate among scientists and engineers on exactly how they were built. What we do know is that the first one in Egypt was built in Saqqara and was designed to be the burial tomb of King Djoser. This massive stone structure was constructed about 2650 B.C. and consists of six distinct levels or steps. We know that the architect responsible for its construction was named Imhotep. Not much is known about his personal life, but he must have been wise. In addition to designing buildings, he served as an astronomer, a doctor, and a high priest.

A GREEK REVIVAL

The art and science of architecture have come a long way in the almost 5,000 years since the first pyramids were built. New building techniques and new materials have allowed modern

The earliest example of a step pyramid is the Pyramid of (Pharaoh) Djoser in an ancient Egyptian burial ground called Saqqara. It was built during the twenty-seventh century B.C.

Today's modern architecture is often inspired by that of the ancient Greeks, including their use of columns. Architecture was among the many areas of interest that flourished in ancient Greece, resulting in such extraordinary structures as the Parthenon.

architects to design tall, sleek structures without the need for a broad base. As it turns out, many modern elements of architecture were first put into practice in ancient Greece.

Greek society was very different from that of societies that came before it. For one thing, the Greeks believed in a democratic process, in which people had a say in how the government was run. As a result, the people of Greece weren't there merely to serve their king or pharaoh. They were free to explore other areas of interest. Philosophy, poetry, music, literature, sculpture, and architecture all flourished. Ancient Greek architecture reached its peak between 500 and 350 B.C. During this time, some of the most impressive structures were built, including the Parthenon and the Temple of Artemis.

One thing unique about classic Greek architecture was its use of columns. Some previous cultures had used columns on a limited basis, but the Greek architects raised their use to a fine art. A **column** is a vertical support element similar to a post. It is designed to hold up horizontal pieces known as **beams** and **lintels**. Almost every structure in ancient Greece had columns. In designing a structure with columns, one of the most important factors that an architect must consider is how they will react to **compression**. Compression is a squeezing force. When an object gets compressed, it usually gets shorter and fatter. In **Experiment 20:** *How Column Shape Affects Weight Support*, you will test several column designs to see how they stand up to the force of compression.

How Column Shape Affects Weight Support

Topic

Does the shape of a column affect the amount of weight that it can support?

Introduction

Over the years, architects have come up with a number of clever ways to support the walls and roof of a building. In ancient Greece, the most common way was to use columns. For a column to work, it must withstand the force of compression created by the weight of the building above it. With few exceptions, almost all of the columns that Greek architects used had circular cross sections. Did they select circular columns because they liked the way they looked, or was there a practical reason? In this activity you will test the strength of three columns of different shapes to see if which, if any, provides a structural advantage.

Time Required

45 minutes

Materials:

- 3 pieces of standard copier paper (8 ½ in. x 11 in.)
- scissors
- roll of cellophane tape
- table
- 10 square wooden building blocks (the type of blocks found in pre-school and kindergarten classes) each 2 ¾ in. x 2 ¾ in. x 1 ¼ in. (7 cm x 7 cm x 3 cm)
- ruler
- pencil

> **Safety Note** No special safety precautions are needed for this activity. Please review and follow the safety guidelines before proceeding.

Procedure:

Part A: Building the Columns

1. Turn a piece of paper so that the long side is vertical (the way that you would normally read a page of text). Measure the following distances down from the top of the page and mark the points with a pencil: 2 ½ in. (6 cm), 5 in. (13 cm), 7 ½ in. (19 cm), and 10 in. (25 cm). Use the ruler to draw a horizontal line parallel to the top of the page at each of the marks. Carefully fold the paper at each line so that you have four panels of equal width, and a 1-in. (2.5 cm) tab at the bottom. Make the four panels into the shape of a square and fold the tab so that it overlaps the last panel. Use the cellophane tape to connect the tab to the panel by taping along the entire seam.

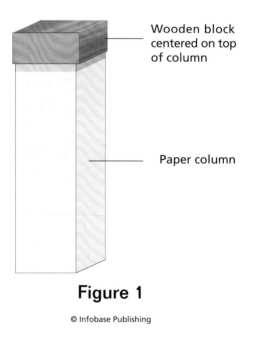

Wooden block centered on top of column

Paper column

Figure 1

2. Take another piece of paper and turn it as you did in Step 1. Measure the following distances down from the top of the page and mark the points with a pencil: 2 ½ in. (6 cm), 5 in. (13 cm), 7 ½ in. (19 cm), and 8 ½ in. (21.5 cm). Use the ruler to draw a horizontal line parallel to the top of the page at each of the marks. Use the scissors to cut off the

paper at the 8 ½-in. mark. Carefully fold the paper at each line so that you have three wide panels and a 1-inch tab. Make the three panels into the shape of a triangle and fold the tab so it overlaps the last panel. Use the cellophane tape to connect the tab to the panel by taping along the entire seam.

3. Take the last piece of paper and turn it as you did in Step 1. Measure 8 in. (20 cm) and 9 in. (23 cm) down from the top of the page and mark the points on the paper. Draw a horizontal line parallel to the top of the page at each mark. Use the scissors to cut off the paper at the 9-in. mark. Roll the paper into the shape of a circle. Overlap the end of the paper by 1 in. so that the end of the paper lines up with the pencil line. Use the cellophane tape to seal the entire seam.

Part B: Testing the Columns

4. Place the column with the square cross-section on end on the table. Make sure that the four sides of the column are not bent in any way. Gently place one wooden block on top of the column and observe what happens. Add a second block on top of that and keep adding blocks until the column collapses. Record the number of blocks that the column held before it collapsed. Repeat the procedure with the triangular column and the circular column.

Data Table 1	
Number of blocks supported by square column	
Number of blocks supported by triangular column	
Number of blocks supported by circular column	

Analysis

1. Which column supported the greatest number of blocks?
2. Which column was the second strongest?

3. What happened to the square and triangular columns right before they collapsed?

4. Which column provided the greatest amount of support?

What's Going On?

This experiment clearly shows that for columns that are the same size and made of the same material, a circular cross-section provides the most support against the force of compression. When an object gets compressed, it is under stress. It begins to deform or bend. In the case of a column, it gets shorter and fatter. The angular shapes of both the square and triangular columns mean that the forces acting on them will not be the same in every direction. This causes planes of weakness to develop within the column. Once the stress due to compression gets to be too great, the column will fail along one of these planes. Right before the column fails, it usually starts to twist. A column with a circular cross-section has no sharp angles. As the compression increases, the internal forces are spread evenly throughout the column. As a result, it takes much more force to collapse the column.

Our Findings

1. The circular column held the most blocks.

2. The triangular column was the second strongest.

3. The square and triangular columns both began to twist before they collapsed.

4. The column with the circular cross-section provides the best support against compression.

FEELING TENSE

In the previous experiment, we saw how too much compression acting on a vertical column would eventually lead to its failure and collapse. For a horizontal beam or lintel, the force of compression is only half the problem. Beams also have to stand up to stresses caused by **tension**. Tensional forces act to stretch an object. In **Experiment 21:** *How Tension and Compression Affect a Beam*, you will explore how a horizontal beam behaves when it is subjected to both tension and compression.

Roofs are held up using beams, which are the horizontal pieces of wood in this roof frame. Beams have to stand up to the stresses caused by both tension and compression.

How Tension and Compression Affect a Beam

Topic

How do the forces of tension and compression affect a beam?

Introduction

Beams are critical construction elements found in most modern structures. A beam is a horizontal support designed to hold up a roof, a deck, or a wall. It is not clear when beams were first put into use, but archaeological evidence suggests that people have been including them in buildings for more than 6,000 years. For a beam to be effective, it must support a large weight, or load, without breaking. Whenever a load is placed on a beam, the beam undergoes stress and begins to change shape. The two forces responsible for this change are called tension and compression. In this experiment, you are going to test a simple beam to see how these forces affect it.

Time Required

45 minutes

Materials

- enough books to produce 2 equal stacks about 12 in. (30 cm) high
- yardstick or meterstick
- 2 cans of vegetables or soup, each weighing approximately 1 lb (450 g)
- ruler
- table
- large ball of modeling clay

Safety Note No special safety precautions are needed for this activity. Please review and follow the safety guidelines before proceeding.

Procedure:

1. Mold the clay into a rectangular prism. As with any prism shape, it should have one dimension longer than the other two. Lay the clay prism on a table so that the long axis is horizontal. Place your hands on either end of it. (See Figure 1.) Slowly bring your hands toward each other and observe what happens to the clay.

Clay prism

Figure 1

© Infobase Publishing

2. Reshape the clay into a prism and repeat the procedure. This time, use your fingers to gently pull the two ends of the clay apart. Observe what happens to the clay.

3. Arrange two stacks of books to be the same height. Place the stacks 12 in. (30 cm) apart. Place the yardstick across the books so that it is centered between them. The yardstick will represent the beam.

4. Use the ruler to measure the distance from the center of the yardstick to the table and record it on the data table. (See Figure 2.) Balance one can of vegetables on top of the yardsick at the midpoint. Observe what happens to the yardstick. Measure the distance from the center of the yardstick to the table top and record it on the data table. Place the second can on the yardstick next to the first. Observe what happens to the stick when additional weight is added.

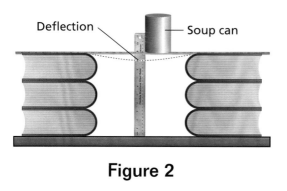

Figure 2

© Infobase Publishing

5. Remove one can from the yardstick, and reset the books so they are 18 in. (45 cm) apart. Measure the distance from the center of the yardstick to the table and record it on the data table. Repeat the procedure twice more with the books spaced 24 in. (60 cm) and 30 in. (75 cm) apart.

Data Table 1	
Starting height of beam Center height of beam at 12 in. (30 cm) with one can	
Center height of beam at 12 in. (30 cm) with two cans	
Center height of beam at 18 in. (45 cm) with one can	
Center height of beam at 24 in. (60 cm) with one can	
Center height of beam at 30 in. (75 cm) with one can	

Analysis

1. What happened to the clay prism when you squeezed the two ends together? What force was this? What happened to the clay prism when you pulled the two ends apart? What force was this?

2. What happened to the yardstick when you put the one can on top? What happened when you increased the weight by adding the second can?

3. What happened to the yardstick when you moved the books farther apart?

4. Based on your observations, why do architects design walls with regularly spaced support posts?

 ## What's Going On?

When a horizontal beam is supported under its two ends, the weight of the beam itself, coupled with any load that is placed on top of it, causes the beam to experience the forces of tension and compression. As the beam sags in the middle, the top of the beam becomes compressed, while the bottom of the beam stretches. As the bottom of the beam stretches, tiny cracks form. If the force of tension becomes too great, the cracks can widen and cause the beam to fail.

The forces of tension and compression acting on a beam can be changed in two ways. One is by increasing the load. When architects design a building, they have to consider not only the weight of the building materials themselves, but also any additional load. This extra load can include people, furniture, goods being stored in the building, and snow and ice that may pile up on top. The second way that the forces on a beam can increase is by changing the spacing of the supports beneath the beam. As the spacing increases, the tension along the bottom of the beam also increases. When architects design walls and roofs, they must make certain that the support structures are close enough so that the beam does not fail.

Our Findings

1. When the clay prism was squeezed together, it got shorter and fatter. This was compression. When the clay prism was pulled apart, it got longer and skinnier. This was tension.

2. When the weight was placed on the yardstick, it began to bend in the middle. Adding more weight made the yardstick bend even more.

3. The greater the distance between the support books, the more the yardstick bent.

4. Regularly spaced supports are needed beneath beams to keep them from sagging and eventually breaking.

MODERN CONSTRUCTION WITH BEAMS

Today's buildings don't look much like the temples of ancient Greece. Buildings of the past tended to be short and wide, while modern skyscrapers are tall and slender. Even though their outward appearance may be different, both types of buildings use many of the same construction techniques. The main difference controlling their "look" lies in the materials used to make them. In the ancient world, most of the heavy construction was done with stone. Stones are great for stacking and stand up to the force of compression fairly well. That's why they make great columns. When stones are used horizontally, however, the force of tension makes them crack quite easily. This happens because stone is not very elastic. **Elasticity** is the property of a solid that allows it to stretch when a force is applied and to return to its original shape when the force is removed. In order for a stone to be used as a beam or a lintel, it has to have many closely spaced upright supports beneath it. This is why most of the large buildings of ancient Greece featured many columns.

Instead of working with stone, modern architects design buildings with steel frameworks. Steel is much more elastic than stone. Pound for pound, steel stands up to the forces of tension and compression much better. This means that a building constructed with steel will weigh much less than a comparably sized building made of stone. Less weight means a lighter load on the beams, so buildings can be built taller and with smaller bases.

Spanning the Globe

As we saw at the end of the last section, architects have always faced a big challenge when it comes to spanning the space between upright support structures. Over time, the constant tug of gravity, coupled with the forces of

Rome's Colosseum is an example of the ancient use of arches. Architects began using arches in construction during the Roman Empire as an alternative to beams, which crumbled over time under the force of gravity as well as the stresses of compression and tension. An arch, on the other hand, is actually held together by compression.

compression and tension, cause beams and lintels to sag and snap. To get around this problem, Roman architects began using a different approach. Rather than using flat beams, they turned to the **arch**. An arch is a curved structure that uses a series of wedge-shaped pieces that lock together to bridge an opening. In **Experiment 22:** *How an Arch Supports a Load*, you will try your hand at some of the same ancient architecture that helped build the Roman Empire.

EXPERIMENT 22

How an Arch Supports a Load

Topic

How does an arch support a load across an opening?

Introduction

An arch allows architects to span much greater distances than they can with simple beams or lintels. Evidence suggests that the first stone arches were built by the Sumerians around 3500 B.C. Egyptian, and Greek architects also experimented with arches, but they weren't used extensively until Roman times. In this activity, you will build a simple Roman-style arch to discover how it uses the force of compression to stand up to gravity.

Time Required

60 minutes

Materials

- 20 to 25 sugar cubes, all the same size
- table
- 2 sheets of cardboard, each 6 in. x 6 in. (15 cm x 15 cm)
- metric ruler
- pencil
- coarse sandpaper (60 grit)
- nail file
- person to assist you

Safety Note No special safety precautions are needed for this activity. Please review and follow the safety guidelines before proceeding.

Procedure

1. Create a stack of sugar cubes that is eight cubes high. Stack the cubes directly on top of one another. Build another tower of eight cubes, but off-set each cube slightly from the one below it. Your second tower should look like Figure 1. Observe what happens to the second tower as you continue to stack the cubes.

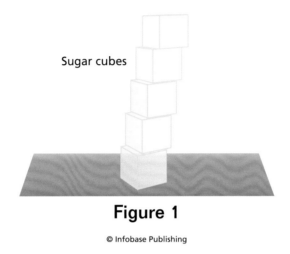

Sugar cubes

Figure 1

© Infobase Publishing

2. Select 11 other cubes. Use the pencil and ruler to mark diagonal straight lines on two faces of each cube so that they have the dimensions shown in Figure 2. You will be reshaping these cubes so that the fronts and backs resemble trapezoids. Lay the sandpaper on the table, rough side up, and then slowly rub each cube on the sandpaper to remove the excess sugar from two sides of the cube. Do not sand past the pencil lines. Use the nail file to do the final sanding on the edges.

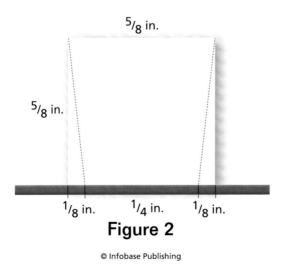

$^5/_8$ in.

$^5/_8$ in.

$^1/_8$ in. $^1/_4$ in. $^1/_8$ in.

Figure 2

© Infobase Publishing

3. After reshaping the cubes, begin constructing an arch by laying the blocks on one piece of cardboard as shown in Figure 3. When you have constructed the arch, lay the second piece of cardboard on top of it so the sugar is sandwiched between the two sheets of cardboard. While holding the two sheets of cardboard together, slowly tilt the arch so it is standing upright. This part is usually easier if you have someone assist you. Once the arch is standing, observe how it is being held together.

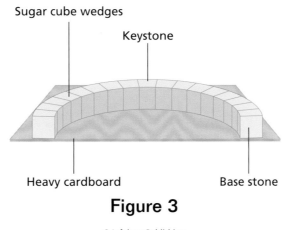

Sugar cube wedges

Keystone

Heavy cardboard

Base stone

Figure 3

© Infobase Publishing

Analysis

1. What happened to the sugar cubes as you stacked them in the first tower? What happened to the second tower as you stacked the cubes? Why?

2. What force held the blocks of the arch together? Why didn't the arch behave like the tower you built out of sugar cubes in Step 1?

3. Why is the top block in an arch called a keystone?

 ## What's Going On?

In order for any structure to remain standing, the weight near the top must be balanced over the point or points of support on the bottom. If blocks are piled directly on top of one another, all of the weight rests on the lowest block. If the blocks are stacked evenly, the tower should remain standing because the center of gravity of the tower is directly over the point of support. When the blocks are offset, the tower leans and quickly falls. The center of gravity is no longer above the point of support. An arch solves this problem by having two points of support that divide the weight equally between them.

An arch is held together by the force of compression. Because each block has a cross-section shaped like a trapezoid instead of a square, each successive block spreads some of the weight to the two blocks on either side of it. One of the most important elements of an arch is the keystone. This is the center block at the top of the arch. It locks all the other blocks in place. As the force of gravity pulls down on the arch, all of the blocks are compressed evenly, and the weight is eventually distributed over the two end pieces. For an arch to work, the base needs to be strong enough to support the weight of the arch above it. The base also has to be massive enough to stand up to the lateral thrust of the two spans pushing out. When you built your sugar cube arch, you probably noticed that it had a tendency to bow out at the bottom. To get around this problem, architects generally make the lowest blocks wider and heavier than those at the top.

Arches are not found only in ancient structures. They are still being used today in many types of construction. Some modern arches are made of stone, but more frequently they are built from brick, steel, and concrete. Arches are particularly important in the construction of bridges and tunnels. Freestanding arches, such as the Arch de Triomphe in Paris and the Gateway Arch in St. Louis, have turned the shape of the arch into a piece of artwork.

Our Findings

1. As the sugar cubes were stacked higher, the first tower may have begun to wobble, but it should have remained standing. The second tower should have tipped over after five or six cubes were stacked.

2. The arch is held together by compression. It didn't fall because it was supported by two sides instead of one.

3. The keystone locks the other stones of the arch in place.

ARCHES, VAULTS, AND DOMES

As the Roman Empire expanded, the idea of using arches in construction quickly spread around the world. For almost 2,000 years, architects used arches in their designs; arches can be found in some of the world's most famous structures. While arches are great for support, they are essentially two-dimensional structures. A single arch is broad and tall but basically flat. To use an arch in a building, you need to line up a number of them. Architects would often connect rows of arches to make an enclosed passageway called an arcade. During the Middle Ages, the use of multiple arches reached its peak with the design and construction of many of the great cathedrals of Europe. Most of these structures have high pointed ceilings called **vaults,** supported by numerous stone arches. To keep the arches from bowing out on the bottom, massive support structures called buttresses were added to the outside of the buildings.

If you rotate the base of an arch in a circle, you get a three-dimensional structure called a dome. Like a vault, a dome

Bridges, like the Navajo Bridge at the Colorado River (above), are often made with trusses, or a rigid framework of beams made with a series of diagonals that turn the framework into a series of triangles. Triangle-shaped framework can support a heavier load than square shapes can because of the way triangles "spread out" the weight of the load.

makes an ideal ceiling for a large open structure. A dome needs no internal support. Like an arch, all of the support comes from downward compression and outward thrust of the dome material itself. One of the first large buildings to have a domed roof was the Pantheon in Rome. Like the arch, domes also spread around the world and they can be found in many historical buildings, including the Taj Mahal in Agra, India, and the U.S. Capitol in Washington, D.C.

TRIANGLES, TRUSSES, AND SQUARES, OH MY!

By now, you have probably figured out that geometry plays a huge role in architecture. From the massive rectangular stones found in the pyramids to the trapezoidal blocks that support arches and domes, the shapes of building elements are critical when it comes to the support of a structure. For example, many bridges have triangles and arches, but few have squares. Many modern structures include trusses in their design. A **truss** is a rigid framework of beams and girders that usually includes a series of diagonal supports. These diagonals turn the square framework into a series of triangles. In **Experiment 23: *Triangular Supports***, you will discover why a simple triangle can work wonders when it comes to supporting a heavy load and why it is often the shape of choice when it comes to designing bridges and buildings.

EXPERIMENT 23 — Triangular Supports

Topic

Do triangular supports hold a greater load than rectangular ones?

Introduction

When Roman architects built bridges and large buildings, they generally used stone arches to support the structure. An arch is really nothing more than a large triangle with curved sides. Later, when iron and steel beams were introduced as building materials, architects found that they needed to add diagonal cross-bracing to the walls of the structure in order to provide maximum support. When diagonal cross-bracing is added to a square, it makes a series of triangles. In this activity, you are going to test two different support systems—one using triangles and the other using squares—to determine if triangular building elements are better at supporting a load.

Time Required

60 minutes

Materials

- 150 round long toothpicks
- 100 miniature marshmallows
- table
- piece of thick cardboard, 12 in. x 12 in. (30 cm x 30 cm)
- ruler
- scissors
- 5 wooden building blocks or similarly sized pieces of wood, each 2 ¾ in. x 2 ¾ in. x 1 ¼ in. (7 cm x 7 cm x 3 cm)

> **Safety Note**   No special safety precautions are needed for this activity. Please review and follow the safety guidelines before proceeding.

Procedure

1. Using the tooth picks and miniature marshmallows, construct four cubes and four tetrahedrons, following the design shown in Figure 1. When building the structures, try to use marshmallows that are all the same size.

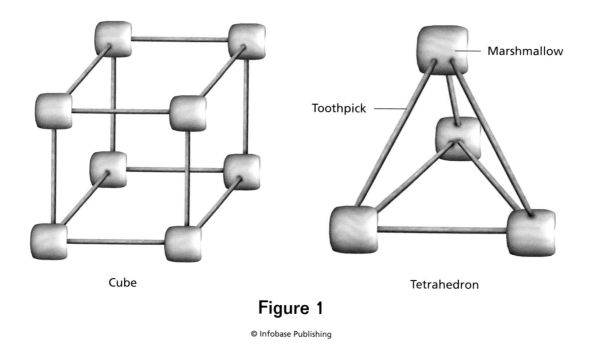

Figure 1

© Infobase Publishing

2. Space the four cubes on a table in front of you so that one cube is under each corner of the cardboard sheet. Rest the cardboard sheet on top of the four cubes and observe what happens. Take one wooden building block and place it on the center of the cardboard while observing the cubes below. Continue adding building blocks until the cubes collapse. Record the number of blocks that the squares could support.

3. Remove the four cubes and repeat the procedure using the four tetrahedrons to support the cardboard sheet. Observe what happens to the tetrahedrons when the load is applied.

4. Cut 24 toothpicks to 1 ¾ in. (4.5 cm) long. Use the shortened toothpicks to construct two cubes with the marshmallows as you did in Step 1. Using longer toothpicks, add diagonal bracing to the sides of one of the cubes so that it looks like the cube in Figure 2. Set the two cubes next to each other on the table in front of you, and rest one wooden building block on top of each cube. Observe what happens to the cubes.

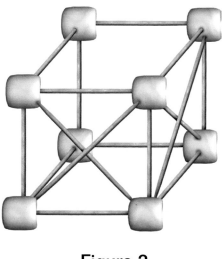

Figure 2

© Infobase Publishing

Analysis

1. Which structures provided more support—the cubes or the tetrahedrons?
2. As you placed the wooden blocks on top of the cardboard sheets, what did the cubes begin to do? What did the tetrahedrons do?
3. How did the diagonal bracing help support the load on the cube in Step 4?

 ### What's Going On?

When a load is placed on a structure, the individual building elements are subject to the forces of tension and compression. Tension happens when an object is pulled apart or stretched, whereas compression happens when an object is squeezed. When a load is placed on a horizontal beam supported by vertical posts (a square), the top of the beam becomes compressed and the bottom is stretched. These two forces cause the beam to slide at its points of support, producing what is known as a shear. If the load is big, the shear will become so great that the beam will pull free from its support and the structure will fail.

Triangles are not subjected to the same shearing as squares because of the way they share the load. When a triangle is compressed from the top, the force is transferred down the sides to the base of the triangle. Although tension occurs along the horizontal base of the triangle, it generally equals the compression along the sides, so the two forces balance. This process is why many large structures will often have tetrahedral piers supporting them at the base. Adding diagonal cross-bracing to the beams that hold up ceilings and floors divides the structure up into a series of small triangles. This dividing helps to spread the load and greatly reduces the amount of shearing.

Our Findings

1. The four tetrahedrons provided much greater support than the four cubes.
2. Before the cubes collapsed, they began to twist under the load of the blocks. The tetrahedrons kept the same shape.
3. The diagonal cross-bracing kept the cube from twisting when the load was applied.

BUILDING BRIDGES

Early people didn't have a great need for bridges. When they came upon a river that needed to be crossed, they either found a shallow area at which they could wade across, or they simply swam. Along routes over which goods and materials were transported, enterprising individuals or the local government set up ferries. When bridges were built, they were usually very simple structures.

This all changed with the rise of the Roman Empire. As the Roman legions moved out across the continent, they had to transport men and material in an efficient manner. To do this, they built many roads and bridges. As previously noted, Roman architects made extensive use of stone arches to support most of the larger bridges. Stone arch bridges are strong and last a long time. In fact, many of the bridges built by Roman architects throughout Europe are still standing almost 2,000 years later.

There are some drawbacks to building a bridge entirely of stone. First, it requires a great deal of material. If there was no rock quarry nearby, the stones would need to be moved great distances. This can be expensive and time consuming. Second, as you probably discovered in **Experiment 22: *How an Arch Supports a Load,*** if the stones do not fit together precisely, the entire structure can come crashing down. In an effort to save time and money, engineers and architects went back to building bridges using wooden timbers. Later, they used iron beams. In some cases, their designs were very successful; others met with disaster. In **Experiment 24: *How Bridge Shape Affects Supported Load,*** you will have the opportunity to test two different bridge designs to see which is better at supporting a load.

EXPERIMENT 24

How Bridge Shape Affects Supported Load

Topic

How does the shape of a bridge affect the amount of load that it can support?

Introduction

When Roman architects built bridges, they generally used stone arches to support them. After the fall of the Roman Empire, architects in Europe and later in America went back to building bridges using a simpler post-and-beam construction. These bridges usually proved adequate for carrying foot traffic, horses, and wagons. After the invention of the railroad, however, things changed dramatically. Many of these bridges could not stand up to the forces created by a fully loaded train. More than a few collapsed. The problem was solved in the late 1800s with the development of the truss bridge. In this activity, you will compare a simple truss bridge to a more traditional post-and-beam bridge to see which is more effective at carrying a load.

Time Required

60 minutes

Materials

- 150 long round toothpicks

- 100 miniature marshmallows

- table

- ruler

- 4 large books, all about the same thickness

- 3 wooden building blocks or similarly sized pieces of wood, each 2 ¾ in. x 2 ¾ in. x 1 ¼ in. (7 cm x 7 cm x 3 cm)

Safety Note   No special safety precautions are needed for this activity.
Please review and follow the safety guidelines before proceeding.

Procedure

1. Using the tooth picks and miniature marshmallows, construct a simple post-and-beam bridge structure following the pattern in Figure 1. When building the structure, try to use marshmallows that are all the same size.

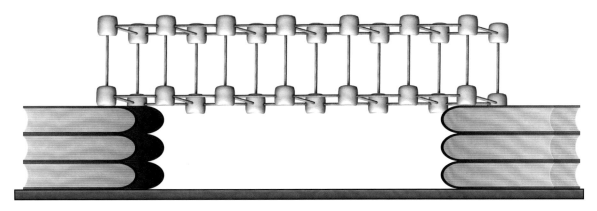

Figure 1

2. Make two stacks of books and space them about 8 in. (20 cm) apart. Carefully center the post-and-beam bridge on top of the books. Allow the bridge to stand for one minute and observe what happens to the bridge span. Place one of the wooden building blocks on top of the bridge at the center of the span and observe what happens to the bridge. If the bridge remains standing, add a second block, and then a third. When you are finished, remove the bridge.

3. Construct a truss bridge with toothpicks and miniature marshmallows, following the pattern in Figure 2. Place the truss bridge on top of the books and follow the same procedure as in Step 2.

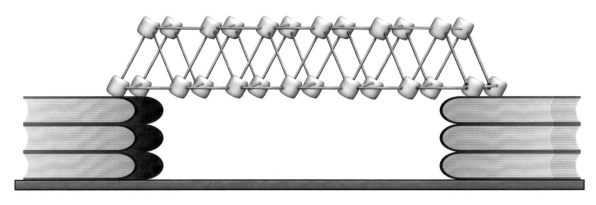

Figure 2

© Infobase Publishing

Analysis

1. What happened to the post-and-beam bridge when you placed it on top of the books?

2. What happened to the post-and-beam bridge when you put a small load on it?

3. What happened to the truss bridge when you placed it on top of the books?

4. Based on your experiment, which type of bridge can support a greater load?

 What's Going On?

Unlike a post-and-beam bridge, which has square or rectangular building elements, a truss bridge is composed of a series of triangular segments. Gravity causes the horizontal beams at the center of a post-and-beam bridge to bend more than the beams over the supports. As a result, the bridge begins to sag in the center. When additional weight is applied, the bridge collapses; shear causes the horizontal pieces either to slip off their supports or to crack. The triangular segments of a truss bridge evenly distribute the weight of load. There are forces of tension and compression, and because these two forces tend to balance in a triangle, much less bending takes place. As a result, the individual support beams stay straight, and little if any shearing takes place.

Our Findings

1. The post-and-beam bridge began to sag in the center.
2. The post-and-beam bridge collapsed as soon as any load was placed on it.
3. The truss bridge remained stable when it was placed on the books.
4. The truss bridge can support the greater load.

SUSPENSION BRIDGES

Truss bridges made of iron and wood work fine, as long as they are relatively short. By the late 1800s, architects and engineers were faced with the challenge of creating longer, stronger bridges. They turned to an ancient design: the suspension bridge. Long before the Romans were building arch bridges made from stone, people were building simple suspension bridges by stringing vines and ropes across river channels and gorges. As the name suggests, a suspension bridge is not held up by supports from below. Instead, it is suspended, or hung, from supports above the bridge deck. One big difference between the suspension bridges of old and today's suspension bridges is the material. Instead of ropes and vines, strong steel cables hold up modern suspension bridges.

Before the late 1800s, high-strength steel really didn't exist. Instead, builders used iron, which is much softer and weaker than steel. Some suspension bridges were built using iron chains to hold up the bridge deck, but these were not stable. The first

The Akashi Kaikyo Bridge is the longest suspension bridge in the world. Suspension bridges have strong steel cables to hold up the roadway.

truly modern suspension bridges were designed by a German-born engineer named John Roebling. Roebling and his son, Washington, revolutionized the design of suspension bridges with the completion of the Brooklyn Bridge in New York City in 1883.

The design of a modern suspension bridge is really quite simple. Two large towers are constructed on either side of a river. Two thick cables made from spun steel wire are anchored to the ground at both ends of the bridge. These are slung over the top of the two towers, and they drop down to the level of the roadway in the center of the bridge. Once the main cables are laid, the bridge deck is built out from the two sides and held up by a series of vertical cables that hang down from the two main cables. These smaller cables are attached every few feet and are designed to keep the bridge stable and to supply extra support.

As materials and technologies continue to improve, suspension bridges also have grown. Some of the most famous bridges in the world are suspension bridges, including the Golden Gate Bridge in San Francisco, the George Washington Bridge in New York City, the Humber Bridge in England, and the Akashi Kaikyo Bridge in Hyogo, Japan. The Akashi Kaikyo Bridge is currently the longest suspension bridge in the world. At 6,529 feet (1,990 m), it is more than a mile long and more than four times longer than the Brooklyn Bridge.

A STRONG FOUNDATION

No matter how aesthetically pleasing a structure is, it is an architectural failure if it doesn't stand up to the forces of nature. One of the most important pieces of any bridge or building design is its foundation. Even though a solid foundation adds very little to the outward appearance of a structure, a building or bridge would quickly turn into a pile of rubble without it. The foundation supports the rest of the structure.

When an architect designs a structure, he or she must consider the type of ground upon which it is being built. Even though Earth itself is made out of rock, there is actually relatively little **bedrock** exposed at the surface. In many cases, the bedrock is covered with sediment. As previously discussed, sediment comes in many sizes and has a variety of properties. Unless a structure is built on solid bedrock, the foundation of a building also needs support. In **Experiment 25: *Spreading the Weight in a Building's Foundation***, you will discover how a **footing** provides support for a building's foundation without having to hit bedrock.

Spreading the Weight in a Building's Foundation

EXPERIMENT 25

Topic

How does the design of a footing provide support for a building's foundation?

Introduction

Over the years, architects have come up with a number of clever ways to support the foundation of a building. In some cases, posts or pilings are driven into the ground until they hit solid rock. In other cases, the overlying sediment is removed to expose the bedrock. Often, a much simpler approach is to build the foundation on top of a structure called a footing. In this activity, you will test to see how the footing below a building can help provide structural support even when there is no bedrock nearby.

Time Required

30 minutes

Materials

- large bag of commercial topsoil or potting soil
- large plastic dish pan
- standard builders' brick
- ruler
- watch or timer
- wooden board about 8 in. x 8 in. x 1 in. (20 cm x 20 cm x 3 cm)
- watering can with water
- garden trowel

Procedure

1. Fill the dishpan about three-quarters full with dry soil. Smooth the surface of the soil with the trowel or your hand, but do not pack the soil down. Measure the depth of the soil, and record this number on the data table. Place the wooden board on top of the soil, centered in the pan. There must be at least 2 in. (5 cm) between the edges of the board and the sides of the dishpan. If the board is too big, remove it, and have an adult cut it to the proper size.

2. Gently place the brick, on its end, close to the center of the board. Observe what happens to the soil as you let go of the brick. After 30 seconds, remove the brick and the board. Measure the depth of the soil that was under the board. Record this number on the data table.

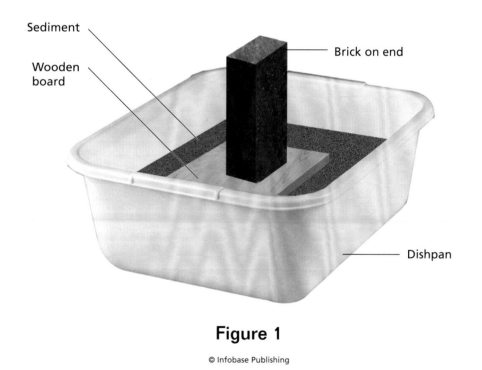

Sediment

Brick on end

Wooden board

Dishpan

Figure 1

© Infobase Publishing

3. Use the trowel or your hand to stir up the soil in the dishpan. Smooth the surface of the soil so that it is the same depth as it was at the beginning of Step 1. Gently place the brick on its end in the soil. Observe what happens to the brick as you let go. After 30 seconds, remove the brick, and measure the depth of the soil that was under the brick.

4. Use the trowel or your hand to remove the soil from the pan and mix it with the remaining soil in the bag. Refill the pan with soil and use the watering can to saturate the top of the soil. Measure and record the depth of the wet soil. Repeat Step 2 with the wet soil and then repeat Step 3. Record the readings of soil thickness for the wet soil on the data table.

Data Table 1	
Initial Depth of Dry Soil	
Depth of Dry Soil Under Board and Brick	
Depth of Dry Soil Under Brick Alone	
Initial Depth of Wet Soil	
Depth of Wet Soil Under Board and Brick	
Depth of Wet Soil Under Brick Alone	

Analysis

1. What happened to the dry soil when the brick alone was placed in it? How did this compare with the soil when the brick was on top of the board?

2. What happened to the brick when it was placed in the wet soil? How did the board change this?

3. In which situation did the soil depth change the most?

What's Going On?

A footing is designed to help support the weight of a building by spreading the weight over a larger surface area. A footing works on the same principle of displacement (Archimedes's principle) that a boat uses to stay afloat. In most cases, the footing of a structure is much wider than the foundation itself. This increase in surface area means that the soil below does not compact as much under the weight of the building. In addition, the footing helps to "even out" variations in the soil that might cause parts of the building foundation to settle at different rates. Evening out these variations keeps the building walls from cracking or collapsing. Footings are usually not made from wood but instead from reinforced concrete that is poured into a form at the building site. When the concrete dries, the footing behaves as one single unit.

Our Findings

1. When the brick was on top of the board, it did not sink into the soil as much as when it was placed on the soil directly.

2. When the brick was placed in the wet soil, it began to tilt. The board allowed the brick to remain straight.

3. The soil became most compacted when it was wet with the brick alone on top of it.

PILING ON

Sometimes a simple footing isn't enough to support a structure. If the soil is extremely soft or if the load is extremely large, architects will turn to **piles.** A pile is like a post driven into the ground to help support a structure. Most modern piles are made of steel or concrete. In the past, most piles were made of wood. Pilings are frequently used to support bridge piers. They also are common under beach houses and boat piers, where the sediment is always shifting.

For the towers of large suspension bridges, piles can't provide enough support. In these situations, engineers use a device called a pneumatic caisson. Resembling a large steel or concrete cylinder with one end open, the caisson is sunk into the river-bed with the open side down. The water is pumped out and air is pumped in, enabling workers to enter it. The workers dig out the sediment below the caisson, causing it to sink deeper into the river bed until it hits bedrock. Then the caisson is filled with concrete, and the bridge towers are built on top of it.

6

What the Future Holds

We've just looked at some of the many ways that humans have explored art and architecture in the past. For more than 40,000 years, people have experimented with different materials and techniques to come up with new and unusual ways of artistic expression. You would think that we would have exhausted the possibilities by now, but human creativity keeps giving us fresh approaches to doing art and architecture. It's hard to know what technological advances will come, but it is certain that both architects and artists will find a way to make use of them. Here are a few recent developments that provide clues as to what is just over the horizon.

DRAWING WITH LIGHT

We previously discussed how the bouncing and bending of light are critical to being able to see paintings, photographs, and even color. These days, artists can go right to the source by actually drawing with a beam of light. If you have ever been to a rock concert, sporting event, or another event at which there was a laser light show, then you've experienced this new art form. Laser light is different from the white light that comes from the Sun or a lamp. Instead of being a blend of different frequencies, laser light waves are all the same. This means that laser light is a coherent form of light.

A second property of laser light is that the rays that make up the beam are parallel to one another. When they leave the laser, they spread out very little. As a result, the light from a laser is extremely bright and can be manipulated to create interesting effects.

Laser light is a coherent form of light. The rays that make up the beam are parallel to one another and spread out very little, making for very bright light that can be manipulated in fascinating ways, such as for laser shows at rock concerts.

Most laser light shows depend on a visual phenomenon called persistence of vision. This is the same effect that allows us to see motion pictures and animated cartoons. In order to produce an image, a laser beam is bounced off several fast-moving mirrors. If the mirrors were stopped, you would see only a single dot. By moving the mirrors, the dot is bounced around so quickly that the individual dots merge into an image. You can try the same effect in a dark room with a bright flashlight. Just shine the beam of the flashlight against a wall or ceiling. Start moving the flashlight around in a circle. The single spot will turn into a circle of light if you get it going fast enough.

Of course, it's a big jump from producing a simple circle of light to the complex images viewed at most laser light shows. Most laser artists rely on a computer to program the images. The output of the computer is connected to an electronic controller with a mirror attached to a swiveling head. The movements and the speed depend on the voltage that the controller receives from the computer. By bouncing the beam off two controllers set at right angles to each other, laser artists can create an infinite number of patterns with a single laser beam.

3-D IMAGES

While we're on the subject of lasers, we can't forget about the science and art of holography. A **hologram** is something like a photograph, only it's a three-dimensional image. It's formed using laser light and is captured on a special photographic plate. Holography is not a new art form. The first holograms were made in the late 1940s, but the technology has developed so quickly that today almost anyone can make them.

When you take a regular photograph, you are capturing light rays on a piece of film. A photograph records the intensity of the light bouncing off an object. The picture will look bright where there is a large amount of light and dark in places with little light. With a hologram, not only are you recording the light intensity, but you also get specific information about the reflected light waves. This information includes the direction and distance from which the light has bounced off the various parts of the object. From this wave data, a three-dimensional image can be constructed.

To make a hologram, light from a single laser is split into two beams. The first beam, called the object beam, is directed toward the object. The object beam is spread out over the object, lighting it. Reflected light from the object then strikes a photographic plate. The second beam, called the reference beam, is directed at the same photographic plate. At the plate, the two beams interfere with each other in such a way that the waves they produce either enhance each other (to make a bright spot) or cancel each other out (to make a dark spot). As the beam scans the photographic plate, an interference pattern of the entire object is produced.

After the hologram is produced, a person can then view the image in regular white light. When you look at a hologram, you are actually seeing hundreds of two-dimensional images, each at a slightly different angle. Because you are looking at the plate with two eyes, each eye sees a slightly different image. It's up to your brain to merge the two images into a three-dimensional image, just as it does when you view objects in the real world.

KEEPING OLD ART LOOKING NEW

One challenge scientists face today is how to preserve ancient pieces of art. Paintings, pottery, and sculptures that are hundreds or thousands of years old are constantly being degraded by the elements. Over time, changes in temperature and humidity, dust, air pollution, and even sunlight can all have negative impacts on various types of art. In most museums, very old and delicate pieces are kept in special climate-controlled cases, and visitors aren't allowed to take flash photographs of the works.

As you might expect, things are even more difficult for art pieces that are not housed in museums. One particularly troublesome problem has developed with the ancient cave paintings found in Lascaux, France. As previously noted, these drawings are thought to be around 20,000 years old. Until a few decades ago, they were incredibly well preserved because the environment in the cave had not changed for thousands of years. Once the cave was discovered in 1940, the internal environment changed quickly. Body heat from tourists, plus the heat from lamps used to light the pictures, raised the cave's temperature. In addition, eager tourists who touched the drawings left behind oils and dead skin cells on the wall, and their breath changed the chemistry of the air.

When scientists realized that leaving the cave open to the public was causing problems, they shut them down in 1963. But the damage was already done. In the late 1990s, scientists started seeing black and white spots on the walls. These were due to several varieties of fungi and bacteria that had been brought into the caves by humans, and they were threatening to cover the pictures. Treating the microbes with a biocide halted their spread, but it didn't kill them all. Recently scientists have discovered that some of the bacteria—which also happen to cause disease in humans—have developed a resistance to the biocide. If the scientists continue using the biocide to protect the artwork, they could be creating resistant bacteria that may someday infect people. If they don't use the biocide, the cave will be overrun with microbes, and the artwork could be destroyed.

ART FROM AUTOMOBILES: RECYCLING AT ITS BEST

Imagine this scene: You're driving along on a rural country road when in the distance you see what appears to be the skeleton of a *Tyrannosaurus rex* towering over the landscape. As you get closer, you discover that the skeleton is not made of bones or plaster casts but instead of wrenches, chains, gears, and a variety of other pieces of machinery. Next to the metal monster is a rocket ship made from pieces of an old Cadillac and what appears to be a giant Fender Stratocaster guitar—only this one is made from real fenders! No, you haven't entered an episode of the *Twilight Zone.* You have stumbled upon Steve Heller's Fabulous Furniture. As you might have guessed, this is not your typical furniture store. Located in the tiny town of Boiceville, New York, (not far from where the famed 1969 Woodstock music festival took place) it is a cross between an amusement park and an old scrap yard.

Steve Heller is not your typical furniture builder. He's an artist who specializes in making "functional art" out of what most people would consider junk. He has been running his shop since 1973, by welding metal, cutting wood, and assembling pieces of old cars into lamps, tables, entertainment centers, and even beds.

Over the years, many artists have "pushed the envelope," trying to find new ways to express themselves. Few have done it as successfully as Heller. He uses many types of old machine parts in his works of art, but the cars that Heller chooses most often as sources for materials are vintage, 1950s-era Cadillacs.

Artist Steve Heller builds art out of old machine parts. His Tyrannosaurus rex includes chains, gears, and wrenches, among other parts.

These cars, which were originally modeled after rockets and planes, feature huge tail fins, bullet-shaped lights, and grills that resemble smiling sharks. Over the years, he has collected dozens of these mechanical marvels, pieces of which can be seen stacked up behind his workshop.

Heller says that creating unusual art forms started when he was growing up in New York City. After he finished his paper route, he would go to a local park and collect oddly shaped tree branches, which he would assemble into "natural" sculptures. His father was an antiques dealer, and Heller would often take some of the broken pieces from antiques and combine them in new ways. This eventually led to his fascination with old automobiles. Rather then see them get crushed, he began rescuing and recycling them into functional works of art. In fact, one of his most prized possessions is the car he drives: a fully restored 1959 Cadillac, complete with side pipes that shoot fire and a variety of his own unique additions.

GLASS HOUSES?

Glass has many properties that give it a variety of uses, including windows, storage containers, and beverage decanters. Though glass is useful, it is also fragile. Hit a piece of glass the wrong way, and it will shatter. For this reason, other than its use in windows, glass was an historically rare building material.

Now, in an attempt to show the strength and versatility of glass, a group of engineers and architects modified the observation deck of the Sears Tower (now called the Willis Tower) in Chicago with four glass observation boxes. The walls, ceiling, and floor of each box are made entirely of glass. Each box sticks out from the side of the building. If people enter a box and look down at the floor, the only thing they see is the street about a quarter of a mile below. The boxes do have a steel framework that secures them to the building, but the glass bears the load. Of course, the glass used in this structure is a bit different from the stuff you find in a typical window or pickle jar. Each structural panel is made of three sheets of half-inch-thick (1.3-cm-thick) glass, bonded together with a polymer film. This unique sandwich approach is designed as a safeguard. If one sheet of glass should crack, the polymer film will isolate it and keep the other sections from breaking.

If the idea of using a substance as fragile as glass as a building material sounds a bit strange, that's exactly what the designers are hoping you will think. They wanted to demonstrate just how far glass-manufacturing technology has come. If they get their way, these structures are just the start. One goal for the future is to eliminate steel and other support frameworks so that a structure can be built entirely of glass. By using special adhesives to hold the glass together, one engineer in Germany has already built a 28-foot (9-m) dome of nothing but glass. Similarly, designer James O'Callaghan has installed glass staircases in all the new Apple Computer stores.

A TRIO OF MODERN DAY PYRAMIDS

There is no question that the ancient pyramids of Egypt and Central America are architectural marvels. At the time of their construction, they were clearly state-of-the-art structures. Although many people think of pyramids as buildings from the past, the design has not faded away. When officials at the Transamerica Corporation wanted a unique building for their headquarters in San Francisco, they went with a

The entrance to the Louvre Museum in Paris contains a vast steel and glass pyramid surrounded by three smaller pyramids. Situated next to the original building, this futuristic structure presents the striking contrast between modern and classical architecture.

pyramid. Completed in 1972, the Transamerica Pyramid tops out at more than 850 feet (260 m) high, making it the tallest building in the city.

When the main entrance of the world-famous Louvre Museum in Paris was in need of a facelift, the architects decided to cover it with an enormous steel and glass pyramid, surrounded by three smaller pyramids. Completed in 1989, the futuristic structure offers an unusual contrast to the classic architecture of the rest of the museum's buildings.

Finally, in 1991 the city of Memphis, Tennessee, built a 20,000-seat sports arena in the shape of a pyramid on the banks of the Mississippi River. Memphis is also the name of a city in Egypt where several important pyramids are located. Rising to a height of 321 feet (98 m), the Pyramid Arena is the sixth-largest pyramid in the world, about 125 feet (38 m) shorter than Egypt's Great Pyramid. What these modern pyramids prove is that some designs can clearly stand the test of time.

GREEN BUILDINGS

These days, you hear quite a bit about "green" buildings, but in this case we're not talking about the color. *Green* is a relatively new term used to describe technologies and structures that have a low impact on the environment. In the past, when architects designed buildings, their main concerns were with the size, function, and stability of the structures. The amount of energy a building was going to use and how much waste it generated were usually afterthoughts. As a result, many traditional buildings use a tremendous amount of electricity for lighting, heating, and cooling. Heating systems that burn oil or natural gas release large amounts of carbon dioxide and other pollutants into the air.

In an effort to reduce the "environmental footprint" of new and existing buildings, many architects are taking a closer look at the structures they design to try to reduce the overall impact they have on human health and the natural environment. They work to reduce the energy that a building uses and to decrease the waste and pollution that it generates. Some green buildings use natural daylight as lighting instead of electric lights. Some have increased insulation in their walls and ceilings, and some have specially designed windows to reduce cooling and heating needs.

Saving energy is only the first step in making buildings green. Some architects have taken their buildings to whole new levels of efficiency by redesigning them from the ground up. By orienting the building in the proper direction, they can take advantage of solar heating and cooling. By using recycled materials in construction, they help to reduce waste. Some architects have even turned their buildings into miniature power plants by incorporating solar panels and windmills that generate a large portion of the building's electrical needs. The bottom line is that the greener a building is, the greener our Earth will be!

ADOBE: AN OLD TECHNOLOGY MAKES A COMEBACK

Every once in a while, a new technological revolution will come along that is not really so new. Take housing, for example. In many parts of the world, people simply cannot afford homes made with lumber, concrete, and brick. This is particularly true in rural desert areas where there are few trees, and lumber and other building supplies must be shipped long distances. To get around this problem, a growing number of architects are turning to adobe, a traditional building material that was first used thousands of years ago. What's adobe? Basically it's mud mixed with straw and other fibrous plant material.

Because it's cheap, abundant, and offers better insulation, adobe is a good alternative to brick or lumber building materials. It is best to use adobe in desert settings because it can fall apart when wet.

Adobe offers many advantages in a desert environment. First, it's plentiful and inexpensive. All you need to do is dig up some dirt, mix it with water and straw, and shape it into bricks. After baking in the sun for a few days, the adobe bricks can be stacked just like oven-fired bricks. Bricks made from adobe are usually much larger than traditional clay bricks. Because of their size, they offer better insulation, which is particularly important when days are hot and nights are cold. Adobe bricks also can be easily shaped to form domed roofs and arched doorways.

There are a few problems with adobe bricks. It is difficult to make the bricks in any color but the color of mud, and they are almost impossible to paint. In addition, when adobe bricks get wet, they tend to fall apart. In a desert, where rain is scarce, this is not generally an issue. In architecture, high technology isn't always the best technology. Sometimes going back to an older, more traditional way of design is the most appropriate technology. That's what the science of art and architecture is really all about!

Glossary

Aesthetics   The philosophy of beauty

Alloy   A metal made by mixing two or more metals together

Arch   A curved structure with interlocking, wedge-shaped elements used to bridge gaps

Architecture   The profession of designing buildings, bridges, and other structures

Artisan   A person skilled at producing crafts, such as pottery, furniture or other useful objects

Beam   A horizontal support in the wall or the roof of a structure

Bedrock   Solid rock that is part of Earth's crust

Canvas   A heavy, tightly woven cloth made from cotton, hemp, or linen on which paint is applied

Clay   This is the finest type of sediment with particles smaller than 0.002 millimeters. Clay is easily molded when wet and turns into a solid mass when dry.

Column   A vertical support element in a structure

Compression   A force that squeezes an object; compression is the opposite of tension.

Ductile   A property of a solid object; a ductile object can be hammered thin or bent into a variety of shapes without breaking.

Elasticity   A property of a solid object; an elastic object changes shape due to a force but returns to its original shape when the force is released. A spring is elastic.

Electromagnetic spectrum   The range of frequencies at which electromagnetic waves will vibrate; the full spectrum goes from radio waves to gamma rays and includes infrared light, visible light, and ultraviolet rays.

Electromagnetic wave   An energy-carrying wave created by rapidly changing electromagnetic fields

Footing   Part of a building foundation located below the ground; a footing is designed to transmit the weight of the structure to the earth

Frequency   The number of times that a wave will vibrate or oscillate in a second

Fresco   A type of painting in which watercolor paints are applied directly to wet plaster

Friction   A force of resistance between two objects when either or both are in motion

Gravity   A force of attraction between objects.

Hologram   A three-dimensional image formed with laser light and captured on a special photographic plate

Kiln   A special high-temperature oven used for baking clay to make pottery

Lintel   A horizontal support over a door, window, or other opening in a building

Malleable   A property of a solid object; a malleable object can be shaped by hammering or rolling

Ore   A rock or mineral that contains metal

Perspective   The science of representing depth on a flat surface

Pigment   A material used in paints and dyes that produces color by reflecting certain frequencies of light

Pile   A post made of wood, concrete, or steel; it is driven into the ground to support a foundation.

Plastic   (adj.) A property of a solid object; a plastic object can be molded.

Proportion   The relative size and shape of objects found in a piece of art or structure

Refraction   The bending of light as it passes from one material to another

Sediment   Small pieces of rock, including sand and clay

Smelting   The process in which metal is separated from ore by heating

Symmetry   When two sides of an object or image can be equally divided by a line drawn through the center

Tension   A force that acts to stretch or pull objects apart; it's the opposite of compression.

Transmit   Pass through

Truss   Rigid framework of beams with diagonal cross members

Vault   An arch-shaped structure usually made of stone or brick; forms the ceiling of a building.

Wavelength   The distance between two successive waves measured from the same point in the wave, either wave crest to wave crest or trough to trough

Bibliography

Chiras, Daniel. *The Solar House.* White River Junction, Vermont: Chelsea Green Publishing Company, 2002.

Dittman, Richard and Glenn Schmeig. *Physics in Everyday Life.* New York: McGraw Hill, 1979.

Hewitt, Paul. *Conceptual Physics 8th Edition.* New York: Addison Wesley, 1998.

Hodges, Henry. *Technology in the ancient world.* New York: Barnes & Noble Books, 1992.

Glancey, Jonathan. *Architecture.* London: Dorling Kindersley, 2006.

Paul, Tony. *How to Mix and Use Color.* Cincinnati: North Light Books, 2003.

Tomecek, Steve. *Bouncing & Bending Light.* New York: W.H. Freeman, 1995.

———. *What a Great Idea! Inventions That Changed the World.* New York: Scholastic, 2002.

Willenbrink, Mark and Mary. *Drawing for the Absolute Beginner.* Cincinnati: North Light Books, 2006.

Further Resources

Barbaformosa. *The Potter's Wheel.* Hauppauge, New York: Barron's Educational Services, 1999.

Baxter, Nicola. *Bridges.* New York: Franklin Watts, 2000.

Bug, Amy. *Forces and Motion,* New York: Chelsea House, 2008

Coakes, Michelle. *Creative Pottery.* Gloucester, MA: Rockport Publishers, 1998.

Glancey, Jonathan. *Architecture.* London: Dorling Kindersley, 2006.

Paul, Tony. *How to Mix and Use Color.* Cincinnati: North Light Books, 2003.

Tomecek, Stephen. *What a Great Idea! Inventions That Changed the World.* New York: Scholastic, 2002.

Wilkinson, Philip. *Building.* New York: Alfred Knopf, 1995.

Willenbrink, Mark and Mary. *Drawing for the Absolute Beginner.* Cincinnati: North Light Books, 2006.

Wood, Robert. *Light Fundamentals.* Philadelphia: Chelsea House, 1999.

Web Sites

Steve Heller's Fabulous Furniture
www.fabulousfurnitureon28.com
This Web site tells the story behind some rather unusual pieces of recycled art. It includes a galley showing many of the pieces created by Steve Heller and his associates at his studio/workshop located near Woodstock, NY.

Holoworld
www.holoworld.com
This site, which is maintained by holography artist Frank DeFreitas, offers a great introduction into the making of holograms. Included in the site is the science behind holography and instructions on how you can make your own holograms.

Stonesharper's "How To" Page

www.stonesharper.com

This site contains all the information you need to get started in making your own sculptures out of stone. Included are sources of materials, descriptions of the tools you will need, and basic directions for actually carving marble and other stone.

M.C. Escher Gallery

www.mcescher.com

This is the official Web site devoted to the life and works of the innovative artist M.C. Escher. Included in the site is a biography of his life plus a gallery showing some of his most famous and unusual works of art.

Green Building: From the Basement to the Roof

www.hgtv.com/hpro/green_building

This Web site provides a great overview of the green building revolution. Included are many helpful articles for both homeowners and building residents. In addition, there is a wide range of videos, which actually show green building practices being put to work.

Picture Credits

Index

About the Author

STEPHEN M. TOMECEK is a scientist who has recently designed his own solar house. He is the author of more than 30 nonfiction books for both children and teachers, including *Bouncing & Bending Light,* the 1996 winner of the American Institute of Physics Science Writing Award. Steve also works as a consultant and writer for The National Geographic Society and Scholastic, Inc.